1050 Questions and Answers in Domestic Science

These questions and answers, all very brief, form excellent revision material for either CSE or GCE O level, or they could be used in class by groups of girls who may finish some assignment ahead of the rest and have a few minutes to fill in.

The main headings are: Nutrition, Food, People, Home, and subsections include such things as money management, safety, personal hygiene, etc., as well as the more obvious topics of cooking and cleaning methods.

The answers are bound in with the questions, but are all together at the back of the book, so that the answer and the question are not both visible at one glance.

Every teacher will have her own ideas as to using the book, but the author stresses that she and "her" girls have a lot of fun with it and that it can be found useful by non-exam as well as exam students.

By the same author

Revision Notes for 'O' Level and CSE Cookery
Safety for your Family
The Young Homemaker (First and Second Books)
Young Homemaker's First Recipe Book
Young Homemakers Second Recipe Book
Young Homemaker's—House and Home
Young Homemaker—Guide to Nutrition
Young Homemaker—Money management
Young Homemaker—Caring for Yourself
Young Homemaker—Looking after Others
Young Homemaker's Sweet and Fancy Cookery
Young Homemaker's Book of Parentcraft
550 Questions and Answers in Parentcraft
Something to Talk About

1050 Questions and Answers in Domestic Science

by Angela Creese

Mills & Boon
London

First published in England by Mills & Boon Limited
17–19 Foley Street, London W1A 1DR

© Angela Creese 1970

Reprinted 1973 (metric measures added)
Reprinted 1975
Reprinted 1977

ISBN 0 263 05420 9

Printed photolitho in Great Britain
by Ebenezer Baylis and Son Limited
The Trinity Press, Worcester, and London

Contents

	Questions page	Answers page
NUTRITION	9	51
General	9	51
Energy	9	51
Carbohydrates	9	52
Proteins	10	54
Fat	11	55
Vitamins	11	57
Mineral Elements	12	61
Meal Planning	14	64
FOOD	17	72
Methods of Cooking	17	72
Meat	17	74
Fish	18	77
Milk	19	78
Cheese	19	79
Eggs	19	80
Cereals	19	81
Fats	20	82
Vegetables	20	84
Fruit	21	85
Stock	21	86
Soup	21	87
Sauces	21	87
Batters	22	88
Réchauffés	22	89
Raising Agents	22	90
Bread-making	23	91
Pastry	23	91
Cakes	24	93
Scones	25	94
Biscuits	25	95
Beverages	25	95
Flavouring Food	25	96
Gelatine	26	97
Convenience Foods	26	98
Preservation	26	99

Definitions	27	102
Failures in Cooking	28	103

PEOPLE	30	107
Babies	30	107
Children—Safety	30	108
Menfolk	32	114
Old People	32	115
Personal Hygiene	33	118
Accidents	34	122
Home Nursing	35	126
Medicine	35	127
Family Safety—Outdoors	36	129
Official Organisations	36	132
Unofficial Organisations	37	135

HOME	38	138
Planning and Caring for the Home	38	138
Safety—General	41	151
Kitchens	44	165
Kitchen Hygiene	45	168
Kitchen Safety	46	171
Laundry	46	173
Money	47	179

Questions

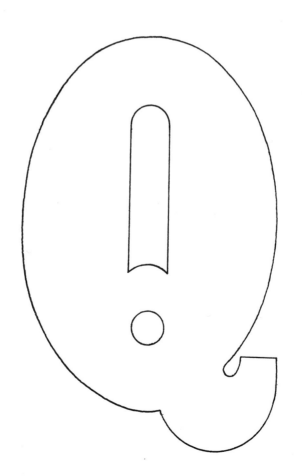

NUTRITION

General

1   Is it true that food may be solid or liquid?
2   Name the three purposes for which the body needs food.
3   What are the names of the nutrients?

Energy

1   Why does the body need energy?
2   How is the energy value of food measured?
3   Give the definition of a Kilocalorie.
4   Is the energy we use for "Work and warmth" measured in Kilocalories too?
5   How many Kilocalories per hour do (a) men, (b) women need for their Basal Metabolism?
6   The amount of energy people require for Basal Metabolism depends mainly on five things. What are these?
7   About how many Kilocalories would the following need each day?
    Man—moderately active.   Woman—moderately active.
    Girl 13–15   Girl 16–20
    Boy 13–15   Boy 16–20
8   If a person eats more food than they need, what usually happens?
9   How can a person lose weight?
10 How many Kilocalories are provided by the following?
    (a) 1 gramme of carbohydrate
    (b) 1 gramme of fat
    (c) 1 gramme of protein.

Carbohydrates

1   Of what main elements are carbohydrates composed?
2   Name the three main kinds of carbohydrate.
3   Sugars are divided into two groups. What are these groups?
4   Name three sugars from each of these groups.
5   Make a list of foods rich in sugar.

6   Briefly describe starch.
7   Make a list of foods rich in starch.
8   Can we digest raw starch?
9   Write brief notes on Glycogen.
10 What is Dextrin?
11 What is Pectin?
12 Write brief notes on Cellulose.
13 Which are the most useful foods for roughage?
14 What is the effect of heat on sugar?
15 What is the effect of heat on starch?
16 Make short notes on the digestion of carbohydrates.
17 Why does the body need carbohydrate foods?
18 Which vitamin must the body have to enable it to digest carbohydrate completely?
19 If we eat too much carbohydrate food, what happens?
20 What is the difference between saccharin and sugar?

Proteins

1   Does all living matter contain protein?
2   Of what main elements is protein composed?
3   What are amino acids?
4   How many amino acids are there?
5   Can the body change some of the amino acids it does not need into the amino acids it does need?
6   Some amino acids are called essential amino acids. Why is this?
7   Name the two classes of protein.
8   Do both these classes of protein contain all the essential amino acids?
9   Is it true that most people need a mixture of protein foods from both classes?
10 Make a list of foods from each of the two classes of protein.
11 Why does the body need protein?
12 Do children need extra protein?
13 Why do expectant mothers need extra protein?
14 Do invalids need extra protein?
15 Describe briefly the passage of protein in the body.
16 What happens to protein when it is heated?
17 What happens to protein when it is overheated?
18 Can the body store the amino acids in protein to use later?
19 Why should carbohydrate foods be eaten with protein foods?

Fat

1 Why does the body need fat?
2 Is fat a more, or less, concentrated energy food than carbohydrates?
3 Can the body store fat?
4 Why are important organs such as the kidneys surrounded by fat?
5 What main elements are fats composed of?
6 Fats and oils consist of two simple groups of substances; what are they?
7 What gives fats, (a) Their particular flavour?
        (b) Their amount of hardness or softness?
8 Some animal fats contain vitamins, which vitamins?
9 Give an example of (a) A soft fat
        (b) A hard fat
        (c) A liquid fat.
10 Do oils become solid if they are cooled?
11 What are the two classes of fats?
12 Make a list of the main fats and fat foods from animal sources.
13 Make a list of the main fats and fat foods from vegetable sources.
14 Is margarine an animal fat or a vegetable fat?
15 What is the effect of heat on fat?
16 Describe briefly the digestion and absorption of fat.
17 Do fats take longer to digest than other foods?
18 Why should fats be eaten with carbohydrate foods?

Vitamins

1 Why does the body need vitamin A?
2 What happens if people don't get enough vitamin A?
3 Which foods will supply the body with vitamin A?
4 Is there more vitamin A in dark green vegetables than in light green vegetables?
5 Can the body store vitamin A?
6 Which groups of people have a special need of vitamin A?
7 Is vitamin A destroyed by heat?
8 Will vitamin A dissolve in water?
9 What is the "vitamin B group"?
10 Will the vitamins of the B group dissolve in water?

11 Why does it make a difference to the body when vitamins dissolve in water?
12 Why does the body need vitamin B_1?
13 Which foods contain vitamin B_1?
14 Which groups of people have a special need of vitamin B_1?
15 What happens if people don't get enough vitamin B_1?
16 What is the effect of heat on vitamin B_1?
17 Is it true that bicarbonate of soda destroys vitamin B_1?
18 Of what use to the body is vitamin B_2? (Riboflavine).
19 Which foods contain riboflavine?
20 Which people need extra riboflavine?
21 What happens if the body doesn't get enough riboflavine?
22 Is riboflavine affected by heat?
23 Is riboflavine lost if milk is left out in the sun?
24 For what does the body use nicotinic acid?
25 In which foods is nicotinic acid to be found?
26 Which groups of people need extra nicotinic acid?
27 If the body doesn't get enough nicotinic acid what happens?
28 Is nicotinic acid affected by cooking?
29 How does the body use vitamin C?
30 Can the body store vitamin C?
31 Which foods are rich in vitamin C?
32 Which groups of people need extra vitamin C?
33 What happens if people don't get enough vitamin C?
34 What is the effect of heat on vitamin C?
35 Is vitamin C soluble in water?
36 How can people make sure they get as much vitamin C as possible from fruit and vegetables?
37 How does the body use vitamin D?
38 What happens if the body doesn't get enough vitamin D?
39 Which foods contain vitamin D?
40 How can the body get vitamin D apart from food?
41 What groups of people especially need vitamin D?
42 What is the effect of heat on vitamin D?
43 Will vitamin D dissolve in water?

Mineral Elements

1 What is meant by the term "Minerals" in nutrition?
2 Why does the body need minerals?
3 Make a list of the chief minerals needed by the body.

4 Why does the body need calcium?
5 Why do children need calcium more than adults do?
6 What happens if children don't get enough calcium?
7 Why do expectant mothers need extra calcium?
8 If old people don't get enough calcium what happens?
9 Name two foods rich in calcium.
10 Make a list of other foods which provide the body with calcium.
11 Is it true that calcium is added to flour?
12 Why does the body need salt?
13 When do people need extra salt?
14 How is salt lost by the body?
15 What happens if the body doesn't get enough salt?
16 What are the main sources of salt?
17 Why does the body need iodine?
18 Which two groups of people especially need iodine?
19 What happens if people don't get enough iodine?
20 List the main sources of iodine.
21 Why does the body need iron?
22 Why do babies need food containing iron after they are a few months old?
23 Which food will give babies the iron they need?
24 Is it all right to give babies and small children tablets or other medicines containing iron?
25 Which other people need extra iron?
26 Does everybody need some iron?
27 What happens if the body doesn't get enough iron?
28 Which foods provide the body with iron?
29 Are there any other useful sources of iron?
30 Can the body use the iron in spinach?
31 Why does the body need phosphorus?
32 Are people very likely to be short of phosphorus?
33 Why does the body need potassium?
34 Which foods contain potassium?
35 Are people very likely to be short of potassium?
36 Why does the body need fluorine?
37 What are the sources of fluorine?
38 Of what use is water to the body?
39 How does the body lose water?
40 What are the main sources of water in the diet?
41 About how much liquid should people drink each day?

Meal Planning

1   What important points must be considered when planning meals for a family?
2   If the family have "plenty to eat" is this good enough?
3   What is a balanced diet?
4   What are the main points apart from nutrition to consider when planning meals?
5   How can meals be made interesting?
6   Should the daily supply of protein food be used all at one meal?
7   In which order should you plan a meal?
8   Is breast milk usually best for babies?
9   Which foods will give a baby the vitamin C it needs?
10   Which foods will give a baby vitamins A and D?
11   How can a baby be given extra iron in its diet?
12   When children have grown out of the toddler stage do they still need vitamins and minerals?
13   Which is the main nutrient children need for growing?
14   Children use a lot of energy; what is the main nutrient they need for this?
15   How important is it for children to have a balanced diet?
16   Which foods are useful for giving children's teeth something to bite on?
17   How much milk should children have each day?
18   Is it important that children's meals should taste nice and look attractive?
19   Should little children be overtired at mealtimes?
20   Is it right for small children to be taught table manners?
21   Should little children have to hurry over their meals?
22   Would you give a small child special cutlery of its own?
23   Is it a good idea to give children small helpings of food to start with?
24   Do you think small children should be given their meals "regularly and punctually" or when they feel like it?
25   Would you give a small child lots of highly spiced food?
26   If children have sweets should they be allowed to eat them just before meals?
27   Is it true that adolescents often need more food than adults?
28   Do teenagers need food for growing?
29   Should teenagers still have plenty of milk?
30   Do most teenagers use up a great deal of energy?
31   Which vitamin will teenagers need plenty of if they eat a lot of carbohydrate foods?

32 Is it important that teenage girls get plenty of iron?

33 Do you think teenagers should have a good knowledge of basic nutrition?

34 What are the main nutritional requirements of expectant and nursing mothers?
Why do expectant and nursing mothers need extra of the following?

35 Protein.

36 Iron.

37 Calcium.

38 Vitamins.

39 Make a list of the foods which an expectant or a nursing mother should have each day.

40 When should an expectant mother start to take special care of her diet?

41 Should she continue to take this care whilst she is feeding the baby and for some time afterwards?

42 If a girl intended to have all her family close together soon after she got married, how would she have to manage her diet?

43 What special points should sedentary workers remember regarding their food?

44 Is it always important for housewives to see that they get the right food?

45 What kind of diet do you think manual workers should have?

46 What kinds of dishes would you include in the diet of manual workers?

47 Why is extra fat useful for people needing a high Kilo-calorie diet?

48 Do old people still need a balanced diet?

49 (a) If old people don't get enough calcium and vitamin D what happens?
(b) What dishes could you give old people to supply calcium and vitamin D?

50 If old people have poor teeth what should be done to make sure their diet doesn't suffer?

51 Should old people have vitamin C every day?

52 Do people still need protein food when they get old?

53 Which protein food is best for old people who have poor digestions?

54 What main types of vegetarians are there?

55 What are the main difficulties in planning meals for strict vegetarians?

56 Which are the most useful foods for vegetarians?

57 Where can advice be obtained on the feeding of vegetarians?

58 What is the first rule for people who want to slim because they are very fat?

59 What are the general rules for slimming?

60 Does it matter which foods go into packed meals?

61 How would you see that packed meals are as nutritious as possible?

62 What other points should be considered when preparing packed meals?

63 What is the first rule regarding the planning of meals for invalids?

64 Which are the important points you should remember when preparing and serving meals for invalids?

65 Does it matter which methods of cooking are used for invalids as long as the food looks and tastes good?

66 If a patient is on a liquid diet what should they be given?

67 Suppose the patient was on a light diet, what would you give them then?

68 When the person is convalescent what foods should they have?

69 Which foods should always be avoided when feeding invalids?

70 Before you go shopping for food what should you do?

71 Is it a good idea to buy large amounts of a food because it is cheap?

72 Is shopping by telephone a good thing?

73 When shopping for (a) meat, (b) fish, how much should you allow for each person?

74 When buying the following vegetables and fruit how much should you allow for each person?
Potatoes, greens, root vegetables, fresh peas and runner beans, fruit for stewing.

75 If you were using the following ingredients in cooking how much would you allow for each person?
Flour for puddings and pies.
Milk for custard and milk puddings.
Soup as a first course.

FOOD

Methods of Cooking

1 Give three reasons for cooking food.
2 What are the main methods of cooking food?
3 Briefly describe stewing.
4 What are the advantages of stewing?
5 Which foods are suitable for stewing?
6 Briefly describe steaming.
7 What are the advantages of steaming?
8 Which foods are suitable for steaming?
9 What are the main rules for steaming?
10 What is the principle of pressure cooking?
11 What are the advantages of pressure cooking?
12 Briefly describe roasting.
13 Which foods are suitable for roasting?
14 Describe braising.
15 Which foods are usually braised?
16 What is grilling?
17 Which foods are suitable for grilling?
18 Make a list of foods suitable for shallow frying and say how much fat you would use.
19 Describe deep fat frying.
20 Which foods are suitable for deep fat frying?
21 Make a list of coatings for fried food.
22 Which fats are suitable for frying?
23 What are the important rules for frying?

Meat

1 Name the chief sources of meat used in this country.
2 What is lean meat?
3 Which meat is tougher, meat from old animals or young animals?
4 Which parts of an animal give the toughest meat?
5 What is suet?
6 Give six points to look for when choosing meat.
7 Give a brief description of the nutritive value of meat.
8 What are meat extractives?

9 Why do we cook meat?
10 Give six ways of cooking meat.
11 Which cuts of beef are suitable for roasting?
12 Which cuts of lamb are suitable for roasting?
13 Which cuts of pork are suitable for roasting?
14 Which cuts of veal are suitable for roasting?
15 How long should you allow for roasting meat?
16 Do thin joints cook quicker than thick ones?
17 What happens to the protein in meat when meat is over-cooked?
18 Which cuts of meat are suitable for frying and grilling?
19 Which cuts of meat are suitable for boiling?
20 Which cuts of meat are suitable for stewing?
21 Which cuts of meat are suitable for braising?
22 Which parts of an animal are called "Offal"?
23 What methods of cooking are suitable for offal?
24 What are the nutrients in offal?
25 When buying fresh chicken what are the points of freshness you should look for?
26 What are the nutrients in chicken?
27 What methods of cooking are suitable for chicken?
28 What are the accompaniments usually served with roast meat?
29 What are the accompaniments usually served with boiled meat?
30 What are the accompaniments usually served with grilled and fried meat?
31 What are the accompaniments usually served with braised meat?
32 What are the accompaniments usually served with stews?

Fish

1 Name the three classes of fish.
2 Does white fish contain fat? If so where?
3 Give the names of some white fish.
4 Give the names of some oily fish.
5 Give the names of some shellfish.
6 How digestible is fish?
7 What are the nutrients in fish?
8 What are the important points in choosing fish?
9 What methods of cooking are suitable for fish?

10 What can be served with fish to make it more interesting and to increase its food value?

Milk

1   Which animal's milk is usually used in England?
2   What are the nutrients in cow's milk?
3   How is milk kept safe before reaching the home?
4   How can milk be kept safe in the home?
5   What different grades of milk are sold?
6   Make a list of the products of milk.
7   What are the points in favour of milk?
8   What are the points against milk? ·
9   Give the uses of milk in the diet.

Cheese

1   Describe briefly how cheese is made.
2   Name some different types of cheese.
3   What are the nutrients in cheese?
4   How can cheese be made more digestible?
5   Which cooking methods can be used for cheese?
6   What are the main uses of cheese in the diet?

Eggs

1   What kind of eggs are used for domestic purposes?
2   What is the composition of a hen's egg?
3   How can you test an egg for freshness at home?
4   What are the uses of eggs in cookery?
5   What methods of cooking can be used for eggs?
6   What care should be taken when using duck eggs?
7   What are the nutrients in eggs?

Cereals

1   What are cereals?
2   What are the nutrients in cereals?
3   From which cereal is flour usually made in this country?

4 What is Semolina?
5 What is Pasta?
6 What is Gluten?
Write brief notes on the following:
7 Oats.
8 Barley.
9 Rice.
10 Maize.
11 Arrowroot, Sago, Tapioca.

Fats

1 What are the main uses of fats in cookery?
Write brief notes on the following:
2 Butter.
3 Lard.
4 Suet.
5 Dripping.
6 Olive oil.
7 Frying and cooking oils.
8 Cooking fats.
9 Margarine.

Vegetables

1 Why are vegetables important in the diet?
2 What are the nutrients in vegetables?
3 Which vegetables are a good source of vitamin C?
4 Which vegetables are a good source of vitamin A?
5 Should vegetables be eaten raw if possible?
6 What is the effect of cooking on vegetables?
7 What points should you consider when choosing vegetables?
8 How can the food value of vegetables be preserved in preparation and cooking?
9 What methods of cooking are used for vegetables?
10 How can you add food value and interest to vegetables when serving?
11 Name three pulse vegetables.
12 How should pulse vegetables be cooked?
13 By what methods are vegetables usually preserved?
14 Name some unusual vegetables.

15 What are the important points in preparing salads?
16 What are the most usual salad dressings?

Fruit

1 Why is fruit an important food in the diet?
2 Which fruits are rich in vitamin C?
3 Which fruits contain vitamin A in the form of carotene?
4 What is the effect of cooking on fruit?
5 Which methods of cooking can be used for fruit?
6 How can fruit be preserved?

Stock

1 What is stock?
2 What is the food value of stock?
3 What should a good stock be like?
4 Which foods are suitable for making stock?
5 Which foods are not suitable for making stock?
6 Name the main types of stock.
7 List the general rules for stock making.
8 If you can't make your own stock what can you use instead?

Soup

1 Why is soup useful in the diet?
2 What are the classes of soups?
3 What are the main ingredients of broths?
4 How are purée soups made?
5 What are the important points of a good soup?
6 What are the accompaniments to:
   (a) Purée soups
   (b) Minestrone?

Sauces

1 What is a sauce?
2 What are the uses of sauces?
3 Describe a good sauce.

4   What are the classes of sauces?
5   Give the proportions of fat and flour for making a sauce using the roux method.
6   Give the proportions of powder to liquid for making a sauce using the blended method. (Pouring and coating)
7   Name several varieties of white sauce.
8   What are the ingredients used for a brown sauce?
9   Name two kinds of cooked egg sauces.
10 Before serving a sauce what should you do?
11 What ingredients are used to make mayonnaise?

Batters

1   What are the main ingredients used for making batters?
2   What is the raising agent in batters?
3   Give the proportions for (a) thin, (b) thick batters.
4   Which thickness of batter is used for making pancakes, Yorkshire pudding and Toad in the Hole?

Réchauffés

1   What does the term "Réchauffé" mean?
2   Give three rules for storing left-over food.
3   Make a list of the rules for using left-over food.
4   When reheating left-overs how can you prevent the food getting overcooked?
5   How can reheated food be made more interesting and nutritious?
6   Give three methods of reheating food.
7   What reheated dishes can be made from left-over meat, fish or vegetables?

Raising Agents

1   If air or carbon dioxide is introduced into a mixture what happens?
2   Give six ways of introducing air into a mixture.
3   How can you introduce carbon dioxide into a mixture?
4   Does water vapour make mixtures rise?
5   What are the ingredients of baking powder?

6 Is yeast a plant or an animal?

7 Is it true that yeast is alive?

8 What are the two kinds of yeast that are used in bread-making?

9 What conditions are necessary for yeast to ferment and produce carbon dioxide?

10 What is the best temperature for working with yeast?

11 What are the conditions which kill yeast?

Bread-making

1 Which is better for making bread, a strong flour or a weak flour?

2 What are the proportions of yeast to flour used in bread-making?

3 Make a list of the usual steps in making bread.

4 If time is short is it possible to leave out any of these steps?

5 Yeast always used to be creamed with a little sugar. Is this still thought to be a good thing to do?

6 Is it true that everything used when making bread should be kept warm?

Pastry

1 What are the main ingredients used in pastry-making?

2 Is self-raising flour ever used for making pastry?

3 What is the raising agent in pastry?

4 What are the proportions of fat to flour for these pastries?
   (a) Suet
   (b) Shortcrust
   (c) Rough puff and flaky.

5 In what way is the fat incorporated in the following pastries?
   (a) Suet
   (b) Shortcrust
   (c) Flaky
   (d) Rough puff.

6 Give seven rules for making pastry.

7 If a recipe says use 4 ozs (100g) of shortcrust pastry, what does this mean?

8 By what methods can suet pastry be cooked?

9 Give two uses of suet pastry.

10 At what temperature should shortcrust pastry be baked?
11 Give two variations of shortcrust pastry.
12 Give several uses of shortcrust pastry, some savoury and some sweet.
13 Why is lemon juice used in flaky and rough puff pastries?
14 Why are the edges sealed when rough puff and flaky pastries are folded during making?
15 Why should flaky and rough puff pastry be left for a while between rollings when possible?
16 At what temperature should rough puff and flaky pastry be cooked?
17 Give several uses of rough puff and flaky pastry, some savoury and some sweet.

Cakes

1 What are the main ingredients used in cake-making?
2 What is the difference between a rich cake and a plain cake?
3 How are cakes usually classified?
4 Name some kinds of cakes which can be made by the rubbing-in method.
5 What temperature should the oven be for rubbed-in cakes?
6 Name some kinds of cakes which can be made by the creaming method.
7 What temperature should the oven be for creamed cakes?
8 What are the general proportions for cakes made by the whisking method?
9 What temperature should the oven be for cakes made by the whisking method?
10 What kinds of cakes can be made by the whisking method?
11 What are the general proportions for making cakes by the melting method?
12 Which ingredients are melted?
13 What temperature should the oven be for cakes made by the melting method?
14 What kinds of cakes can be made by the melting method?
15 How can you tell if cakes are cooked?
16 How long will cakes keep if properly stored?
17 How can you prevent curdling when egg is added to creamed sugar and fat?

Scones

1   What is the usual method of making plain scones?
2   Give the proportions for making scones.
3   At what temperature should plain scones be baked?
4   For how long should they be baked?
5   Give some variations of scones which can be made from the basic recipe.
6   How thick should plain scones be rolled?

Biscuits

1   How are biscuits classified?
2   Are raising agents used in biscuit making?
3   Why are biscuits usually pricked with a fork?
4   Should biscuits be stored in the same tin as cakes?

Beverages

1   What is the food value of tea, coffee and cocoa?
2   Name three kinds of tea.
3   Coffee and tea contain caffeine. What does this do?
4   Tea contains tannin. What does this do?
5   How is coffee sold?
6   Why is cocoa a more suitable drink for children than tea or coffee?
7   Name some proprietary food drinks.
8   What is the value of these proprietary food drinks in the diet?
9   Is there any food value in "fruity drinks"?

Flavouring Food

Write short notes on the following spices:
1   Allspice.
2   Cinnamon.
3   Cloves.
4   Curry powder.
5   Ginger.
6   Nutmeg.

Write short notes on the following essences:
7 Almond.
8 Peppermint.
9 Vanilla.
Briefly describe the following herbs:
10 Bay leaves.
11 Chives.
12 Garlic.
13 Sage.
14 Thyme.

Gelatine

1 What is gelatine?
2 How is gelatine usually sold?
3 What is the food value of gelatine?
4 What are the important points to remember when using gelatine?
5 What is aspic jelly?
6 Which dishes is gelatine used for?

Convenience Foods

1 "Convenience foods are not a recent invention."
   Give examples of some convenience foods which prove this statement.
2 Give some advantages of convenience foods.
3 Give some disadvantages of convenience foods.
4 Write short notes on the buying and storing of convenience foods.

Preservation

1 Why is food preserved?
2 Give four causes of food decay.
3 What are enzymes?
4 Are enzymes harmful?
5 How can the action of enzymes be stopped?
6 What are yeasts?
7 Where are they found?
8 What conditions are necessary for them to grow?

9 What conditions are necessary for:
(a) Yeasts to be destroyed
(b) Yeasts to remain dormant?
10 What are moulds?
11 Where are moulds to be found?
12 What conditions are necessary for moulds to grow?
13 What conditions are necessary to check the growth of moulds?
14 What are bacteria?
15 What conditions are necessary for bacteria to grow?
16 What conditions are necessary:
(a) To destroy bacteria
(b) To prevent the growth of bacteria?
17 Is it true that some bacteria make food poisonous?
18 Name four general methods of preserving food.
19 Which foods can be bottled at home?
20 What are the main points regarding bottling fruit?
21 Write brief notes on canning.
22 What is the most important thing to remember about freezing?
23 Describe briefly what quick-freezing is.
24 (a) What is A.F.D.?
(b) What are its advantages?
25 Give a short description of drying.
26 What is used for chemical preservation?
27 What are the main ingredients for making jam?
28 What is pectin?
29 Name some fruits which are rich in pectin.
30 Name some fruits which are poor in pectin.
31 How can fruit which is poor in pectin be successfully made into jam?
32 How can fruit be tested for pectin content?
33 What is the main rule regarding cooking jam?
34 What are the tests for setting?
35 How should jam be stored?

Definitions

Briefly describe the following:
1 Au gratin.
2 Bake blind.
3 Baste.

4 Blanch.

5 Blend.

6 Bouquet garni.

7 Croûtons.

8 Forcemeat.

9 Garnish.

10 Glaze.

11 Macédoine.

12 Parboil.

13 Roux.

14 Sauté.

15 Zest.

Failures in Cooking

What can cause things like the following to go wrong?

CAKES

1 Sunk in the middle.

2 Fruit sunk to the bottom.

3 Risen too high and cracked in the middle.

PASTRY

4 Short pastry—tough and hard.

5 Rough puff and flaky pastry—tough and hard.

6 Rough puff and flaky—risen unevenly.

7 Pastry shrinking when cooked

8 Suet pastry—tough and hard.

9 Suet pastry—heavy and wet.

BREAD

10 Heavy dough—doesn't rise much the first time.

11 Heavy dough—doesn't rise much after proving.

12 Wrinkled top when cooked.

13 Sour taste.

SAUCES

14 Lumpy.

15 Raw flavour.

16 Lacking gloss.

17 Too thin.

JAM

18 Not set.

19 Fruit risen to the top.

20 Mould on top.

21 Crystallised.

BOTTLING

22 Fruit risen to the top.

23 Moulds formed.

FRYING

24 Too greasy.

25 Black specks on the food.

26 Rissoles, etc., burst.

27 Food raw inside.

GENERAL

28 Egg custard curdled.

29 Junket not set.

PEOPLE

Babies

1   Make a list of the main physical needs of babies.
2   What other important things do babies need?
3   Name the main things babies don't like. . .
4   Is it a good idea to keep to a baby's usual timetable at times like Christmas and birthdays?
5   List the main things that a baby-sitter should know.
6   What are the safety rules for taking babies out?
7   (a) Make a list of the main emotions people feel.
      (b) Do small children feel these things too?
8   What is the difference between the ways small children manage their feelings and the ways really grown-up people manage theirs?
9   Is it true that a person can get very angry with a person and yet still love them? (e.g. parents and children).
10 If a small child is afraid of the dark, should he have a safe night-light?
11 How would you try to prevent a small child being jealous of a new baby?
12 Name some ways in which small children learn.
13 How can you teach small children to become independent?

Children—Safety

1   What can be done to prevent small children falling in the home?
2   How can children be prevented from falling from prams, etc.?
3   In what ways could you prevent a small child falling in the bathroom?
4   Children often trip over their own clothes. What can be done about this?
5   Make a list of sharp things which must be kept away from small children.
6   What can be done to prevent small children being electro-cuted by the following:
      (a) Power points
      (b) Flexes
      (c) Electric blankets

(d) Television and radios

(e) Any other electric appliances?

7 Make a list of things which can poison small children.

8 How can people prevent children being poisoned by such things?

9 Can little children be poisoned by things which don't seem like medicine? e.g. Vitamin tablets, slimming tablets.

10 If coal gas is the fuel used in the home, what precautions must be taken to protect small children from gas poisoning?

11 Is it true that little children can be poisoned by smelling certain things?

12 When are small children most likely to eat poisonous things?

13 Could a baby be poisoned by the ointment or dusting powder put on it?

14 What are the main ways children get scalded?

15 What are the main ways to prevent children being scalded?

16 How can you prevent children pulling the tablecloth so that a pot of tea pours all over them?

17 What are the rules for bathing small children to keep them safe?

18 Should you drink hot drinks whilst holding a baby?

19 How can children be prevented from getting scalded by hot water bottles?

20 How can a child be kept safe from suffocation

(a) whilst sleeping

(b) whilst feeding?

21 A plastic bag can kill a child. How can this be prevented?

22 What would you do to make sure a baby didn't get suffocated by fumes and smoke?

How can children be prevented from being burned by the following?

23 Fires.

24 Candles and night-lights.

25 Matches and lighters.

26 Cookers.

27 November 5 celebrations.

28 Inflammable clothing.

29 Sun.

30 What care should you take if you have to leave your baby with somebody else?

31 What are the rules about hitting children?

32 Do children need to be treated carefully when they are being bathed, dressed, fed, played with?

33 Do little babies do things out of spite or to be annoying?

34 If little babies cry, refuse food, dirty nappies quickly, are sick or stay awake, are they being naughty or "awkward"?

35 Where can young mothers get help if they need it to look after their children properly?

36 What is the name of the association who will look after children if they are ill-treated?

37 What infectious diseases can be prevented these days?

38 How can a mother help to keep her child well?

39 What can be done to prevent small children getting ill from animals?

40 If you really think a child is ill should you ring the doctor at once or wait to see if the child gets better?

41 How can you help to keep a child safe at play?

42 What can you do to make the garden a safe playground?

43 What safety points should you look for when buying toys for children?

44 How can you make sure that toys are safe?

45 What special checks should you make (a) For soft toys
                                      (b) For wooden toys?

46 What can be very dangerous about painted toys?

47 How can you prevent small children getting lost outdoors?

48 What are the rules for crossing the roads with toddlers?

49 How can you keep little children safe on public transport?

50 What is the name of the road safety club for small children?

51 What things can you teach children to keep them safe in most situations?

Menfolk

1   What things in the home are useful for boys to learn?

2   If you were buying clothes for boys what points would you take into consideration?

3   How can wives help to keep their husbands fit?

4   Which are the main organisations that will help with home problems?

Old People

1   How can you help provide for old people's physical needs?

2 What can be done to see that old people get the food they need?

3 If you had to get clothes for an old person, what things would you consider?

4 How would you look after an old person's (a) Hair, (b) Hands, (c) Feet?

5 What jobs can young people do for old people who live alone?

6 If you had an old person living with you, how would you try to make them happy?

7 It is important that old people are kept warm. How can this be done?

8 How can old people be kept safe from burns?

9 What would you do to prevent an old person getting scalded?

10 How would you prevent them getting poisoned by coal gas?

11 Old people fall easily; what can be done to prevent these falls?

12 What can be done to help to keep old people safe on the roads?

13 Is it a good idea to give old people their medicine?

14 What can be done for the safety of old people living alone?

15 Should old people be left in charge of young children?

Personal Hygiene

1 Why is it important to keep skin clean?

2 How should you care for your teeth?

3 In what ways should you look after your hair?

4 What would you do to keep your brush and comb hygienic?

5 What would you teach a small child about nose hygiene?

6 How should ears be cared for?

7 In what ways should you care for your eyes?

8 Make a list of the main points of hand and nail care.

9 How should the feet be looked after?

10 How should you buy and care for footwear?

11 What use is exercise to the body?

12 Why should you take care to cultivate correct posture?

13 How important is sleep to the body?

14 In what ways would you care for your clothes to keep them in a hygienic condition?

15 What points should you consider when buying clothes, apart from fashion?
16 Are fresh air and sunshine good for people?
17 How can underwear be kept fresh and clean?
18 How can you look smart whilst doing the housework?
19 Smart handbags should be kept clean and tidy; how can this be done?
20 "Coughs and sneezes spread diseases." How can the spread of diseases be prevented?
21 How can you get a well-groomed look?
22 Is hygiene important to beauty care?
23 What are the important points to remember about make-up?
24 Is it necessary to use a deodorant every day as well as washing and bathing?
25 If you have a discharge at any time between periods what should you do?
26 How can bad breath be prevented?
27 Some girls are extra tired and a little on edge a day or two before their period starts. Why is this?
28 If you always feel depressed and miserable for no reason, what should you do?
29 How can you prevent unnecessary depression?
30 Make a list of useful teenage hobbies.

Accidents

1 Make a list of the main things which should be in a First Aid box.
2 List several points on the use and care of the First Aid box.
3 How can a family be prepared in case of accident?
4 What must you know to get help quickly in case of an accident?
5 Make a list of the general rules which should be known in case of accidents.
6 How should small cuts be treated?
7 What should you do if somebody gets cut badly?
8 How should you treat a case of nose bleed?
9 How should you treat a small burn?
10 What should you do if a person is badly burned?
11 How should you treat a person who has fainted?
12 If you suspect that a person has broken a bone what should you do?

13 If somebody swallowed something poisonous what should you do?

14 What can you do if somebody is electrocuted?

15 How should you treat mild insect bites and stings?

16 If somebody is apparently drowned what should you do?

17 How should you treat a baby who is having a fit?

18 What is the First Aid treatment for heat stroke?

19 What can you do if a person gets something in their eye?

20 What can you do if a person has swallowed some object?

21 If you found your baby as cold as ice although he looked all right what should you do?

Home Nursing

1 If you have to send a child for the doctor what should you do?

2 If one of the family is ill and you have to be nurse, how would you set about it?

3 What is the most important rule for a home nurse?

4 What rules would you suggest for visitors?

5 If you could choose which room to use as a sickroom what points would you consider?

6 If the doctor asks for a "Specimen" what does it mean?

7 How would you arrange the furniture in a sickroom?

8 What are the main rules for cleaning a sickroom?

9 What are the rules for filling hot water bottles?

10 What things should you put ready for the doctor?

Medicine

1 What are the main rules about using medicine safely?

2 How should you give medicine?

3 Why is it wrong to call tablets and pills "sweets" to children?

4 Is it safe to give or take medicine which has not been prescribed for a person?

5 What should you do with old medicine?

6 What does "For external use" mean?

7 Describe a safe medicine cupboard.

8 How should you use a medicine cupboard?

9 How should you take extra care with aspirins?

10 How should you give or take sleeping tablets?
11 What questions should you ask your doctor about your medicine?

Family Safety—Outdoors

1 Should people read the Highway Code if they don't drive?
2 Should grown-ups and older children obey all the road safety rules when they are out with small children?
3 What are the rules for walking at night?
4 If you are pushing a baby in a pram outdoors what care should you take?
5 What are the main cycling rules?
6 What are the safety rules for travelling by bus?
7 If you are travelling by train what care should you take?
8 What are the main safety rules for drivers of cars?
9 What things prevent people from driving their best?
10 When and where should drivers take extra care?
11 How can children be kept safe in cars?
12 What can drivers do to make sure elderly passengers are kept safe?
13 Which things should be kept in cars in case of accident?
14 What are the main causes of accidents in schools?
15 Make a list of safety rules which would be suitable for work places.
16 Make a list of general safety rules for holidays.
17 Is it a good idea for all the family to be "labelled" when away on holiday?
18 If you go out for the whole day when you are away on holiday what should you make sure you do?
19 Make a list of the main safety rules for swimmers.
20 List the main safety rules for holiday-makers going in boats.
21 When should you ring the coastguard for help?
22 What special precautions should holiday-makers take if they are going climbing?
23 Make a list of safety rules for campers.

Official Organisations

Write brief notes on the following organisations and people:
1 National Health Service.

2 General Medical Service.
3 Supplementary Benefit.
4 Public Health Inspectors.
5 Clinics, Ante and Post natal.
6 Midwives.
7 Health Visitors.
8 District Nurses.
9 Home Help Service.
10 Almoners.
11 School Health Service.
12 Hospital Service.

Unofficial Organisations

Write brief notes on the following unofficial organisations and those who work for them:
1 British Red Cross Society.
2 Citizen's Advice Bureaux.
3 National Society for the Prevention of Cruelty to Children.
4 Order of Saint John.
5 Women's Royal Voluntary Service.
6 Royal Society for the Prevention of Accidents.
7 Royal Society for the Prevention of Cruelty to Animals.

HOME

Planning and Caring for the Home

1   What are the main kinds of homes that people live in in England?
2   How can you find a place to live in?
3   If you are renting accommodation, what things do you need to know?
4   If you have an agreement to sign and don't understand it who will help you?
5   If there is no agreement what extra things must you take trouble to find out?
6   Apart from the price and things the surveyor checks, what things does the buyer need to check up on before buying a house?
7   What things would you need to know about the district before you bought a house?
8   What are the main causes of damp in a house?
9   What is a damp course?
10 (a) What is dry rot?
    (b) How is it caused?
    (c) How can it be prevented?
11 What is damp rot?
12 How can damp rot be prevented?
13 What are the usual types of fuel used to heat houses?
14 How can you keep down the cost of home heating?
15 What does insulation mean?
16 How can a house be insulated?
17 How would you get a house ready for the winter?
18 How can the most use be made of natural light in the home?
19 What are the main kinds of artificial light you can use?
20 What does it mean to keep a house "well ventilated"?
21 Which are the most usual ways of ventilating the home?
22 How can you prevent waste of water?
23 How can you prevent pipes freezing?
24 If you go away in the winter, what should you do?
25 By what methods is water usually heated?
26 How can you look after the hot water system?
27 If the hot water system freezes should you light the boiler?

28 Make a list of the things likely to block a sink.

29 If the sink gets blocked what should you do?

30 Which things are likely to block a lavatory?

31 What should you do to keep drains clean and safe?

32 How should the outside gutterings and pipes of a house be cared for?

33 What points should a home decorator look for in paint?

34 What are the main types of wall covering?

35 How would you prepare a room which is going to be completely redecorated?

36 Make a list of the different types of furniture used in most homes.

37 What are the main types of floor covering?

38 What kind of things do you need to know about a carpet before you buy?

39 What do the names, "Wilton" and "Axminster" mean?

40 Why are underlays important?

41 What does the amount of material you need for curtains depend on?

42 What points would you look for when buying curtain material?

43 Which main points would you look for when buying floor coverings?

44 What are the important points you should consider when planning a room for a baby?

45 If you were planning a room for an old person what would you consider?

46 Apart from the safety aspect what are the main points you should remember when using cleaning materials?

47 Make a list of important points regarding the use of the vacuum cleaner.

48 How should you care for household cloths? (Not bed or table linen).

49 Brooms and brushes last longer if they are properly cared for. How would you do this?

Write brief notes on the cleaning of the following:

50 Non-stick cooking utensils.

51 Non-coated aluminium and tin.

52 Copper and brass.

53 Chromium.

54 Stainless steel.

55 Steel knives.

56 Silver and electro plate.

Write brief notes on the cleaning of the following:
57 White wood equipment.
58 Painted wood.
59 Polished wood.
60 What is "the beetle"? How do you prevent and treat it?
61 What is the general method for cleaning upholstery?
62 Name two ways of cleaning windows.
63 How would you clean a framed picture?
Give the main points for cleaning the following:
64 Carpets.
65 Linoleum.
66 Rubber flooring.
67 Thermoplastic tiles.
68 Vinyl floor covering.
69 How would you clean out a drawer?
70 What are the main jobs which have to be done when cleaning a room out?
Describe briefly the main daily jobs for cleaning the following:
71 Kitchen.
72 Sitting room.
73 Bedroom.
74 Bathroom.
75 Toilet.
76 List some rules for looking after the larder.
77 Make a list of general points for cleaning a gas cooker.
78 Make a list of general points for cleaning an electric cooker.
79 What things should you do when using a refrigerator?
80 What things should you not do when using a refrigerator?
81 What are the general rules for table setting?
82 What are the general rules for clearing the table?
83 In what order should the washing up be done?
84 Describe the correct order for lighting a coal fire.
85 How should you use (a) a pedal bin
                      (b) a dustbin?
86 Make a list of the ways a housewife can save time in cooking.
87 Make a list of the ways a housewife can save time on housework.
88 What are the main points to consider when making daily work plans?
89 How can a housewife use her saved time?
90 If a housewife becomes very lonely, what can she do about it?

91 Make a list of important points which help to make a home run smoothly.

Safety—General

1 If you were planning the building of your own house, what are the chief safety points you would consider?

2 How can windows be made safe?

3 What could be done to make it less likely for a person to walk into a glass door and be cut by breaking the glass?

4 How can stairs be made safe?

5 Where are extra lights needed for safety?

6 What safety points should you look for when buying things for the house or for your own use?

7 Name some bodies of people who try to make sure that the things we use are safe.

8 What is the name of the special label of the British Standards Institution?
What safety points would you look for when buying the following?

9 Furniture.

10 Electric appliances.

11 Gas appliances.

12 Oil appliances.

13 China and glass.

14 Cutlery.

15 Cooking utensils.

16 Soft furnishings.

17 Things for children.

18 What are the safety points to look for in the following:

Fire guards	Hearthrugs
Plastics	Bedside lamps
Christmas decorations	Bolts for bathroom doors.

19 Which household equipment should you use extra carefully to prevent accidents?

20 How would you dress for doing the housework to make sure that your clothes didn't cause you to have an accident?

21 How should you care for all household equipment to prevent accidents?

22 What should you use for climbing jobs?

23 What are the general rules for using cleaning materials safely?

24 What are the safety rules regarding rubbish?
25 How could you prevent accidents from sewing equipment?
26 How can pets cause accidents indoors?
27 How can you prevent pets from causing accidents outdoors?
28 Name some equipment which will help prevent accidents to home handymen.
29 What are the safety rules for using tools?
30 What safety points should a handyman check regarding the materials he uses?
31 Make a list of household repair jobs inside the home which should be done at once.
32 Make a list of outside house repairs which should be done at once.
33 What are the main accidents which can happen through the wrong use of gas appliances?
34 What should you do if you smell gas?
35 What are the general rules for using gas safely?
36 What extra care should you take when using a gas water heater?
37 What are the main rules for using electrical appliances safely?
38 What points should you watch to prevent accidents caused by flexes?
39 What does overloading mean?
40 How can you prevent overloading?
41 Should you take electric fires into the bathroom?
42 How can you keep a safe garden?
43 Which garden jobs should be done regularly?
44 What special care should be taken when using gardening equipment?
45 Children love to play in sheds; how would you make sure they are safe places?
46 Water can be the cause of many drowning accidents in the garden; how can children be protected from such accidents?
47 List the ways in which fires start.
48 There are three main ways in which death can be caused through fires. What are they?
49 Make a list of ways to prevent fire.
50 How can you prevent fires starting from open grates?
51 How should an open fire be left at night?
52 If it's windy how should you make up a fire?
53 What can be done to prevent chimney fires?
54 Which things should never be put on the mantelpiece?

55 What are the main safety rules to be kept regarding oil stoves?

56 Name some inflammable things near which it is dangerous to smoke.

57 What are the main safety rules regarding smoking?

58 When should extra care be taken where people are smoking?

59 Which rubbish is most likely to cause a fire?

60 Which things should never be put on open fires?

61 What care must be taken to prevent garden fires?

62 How should clothes *not* be aired?

63 How would you prevent these things starting fires?
  (a) Lighter fuel.
  (b) Fats and oils.
  (c) Petrol and paraffin.
  (d) Aerosols.
  (e) Polishes and other inflammable cleaners.

64 If any of the family have the following hobbies—chemistry, photography, making aeroplanes, what should you do?

65 Which are the special times of the year you should take extra care to prevent fire?

66 If you had a children's party what precautions would you take to keep the children safe?

67 What are the safety rules for decorating the home at Christmas time?

68 Many fires are caused on Guy Fawkes night by fireworks, etc. What can be done to prevent such accidents?

69 How can you prevent a fire starting when you are out of the house?

70 What precautions should you take before winter sets in to prevent house fires?

71 When the family go to bed at night what care should be taken to prevent fire breaking out?

72 If fire breaks out in a building what is the first rule which must be obeyed?

73 How can fire be prevented from spreading?

74 What fire-fighting equipment can be bought for ordinary homes?

75 Which association will give advice on how to make a home safer from fire?

76 Should you call the fire brigade before a fire gets a real hold on a building?

77 How can you call the fire brigade?

78 Should you call the fire brigade for chimney fires?

79 If a person's clothes catch on fire what should be done?

80 If you think there is a fire behind a closed door should you open the door to look?

81 What should you do if the fat pan catches fire?

82 Is it a good idea to work out escape routes from the house in case of fire?

83 Should families have fire drill at home?

84 If you have a fire extinguisher and it is used what must you do?

85 What can be done to help keep burglars out of the home?

86 What are the safety rules regarding callers?

87 When should extra care be taken to keep the home safe from burglars?

88 What can neighbours do to keep other neighbours' homes safe from burglars?

89 What must you do if you are going away, to prevent burglars?

90 Is there anything you can buy to protect your home from burglars?

91 How can you protect your valuables?

92 How can you keep your valuable things safe whilst you are out shopping?

93 What can be done to prevent cars from being stolen?

94 How can the police help people before trouble?

Kitchens

1 List the important points of a well-planned kitchen.

2 In what ways can a kitchen be planned to avoid undue strain on the housewife?

3 What special points should you consider when buying a cooker?

4 What should you remember when using a cooker?

5 Before buying a sink what should you take into consideration?

6 What care should you take in using a sink?

7 What should you look for when buying a refrigerator?

8 How should you use a refrigerator to best advantage?
   What should you look for when buying the following?

9 Saucepans.

10 Baking tins.

11 Cutlery.
12 Casseroles.
13 Bowls and basins.
14 What are the general rules for buying and caring for small equipment?

Kitchen Hygiene

1 Which floor coverings are most hygienic?
2 How can walls be kept clean and hygienic?
3 What are the best coverings for kitchen ceilings?
4 Why is good lighting important for cleanliness?
5 Bacteria multiply very quickly in warm places. How can this be prevented in the kitchen?
6 How would you prevent your kitchen getting really dirty?
7 What are the best surfaces for kitchen tables, shelves and cupboards?
8 Name some danger spots in kitchens which need regular cleaning.
9 Pests spread disease. How can they be kept out of kitchens?
10 How may food be infected?
11 What are the main points of hygiene regarding shopping for food?
12 What extra care should you take when buying frozen food?
13 List the main rules for storing food.
14 Make a list of rules for people preparing and serving food.
15 If you had a cold and had to prepare the meal what precautions would you take?
16 If food has to be prepared in advance what care must be taken to avoid food poisoning?
17 What is the recommended time and temperature for reheating food to prevent food poisoning?
18 Make a list of easily infected food.
19 Which meat is especially dangerous if eaten underdone or raw?
20 What care should be taken with pet food?
21 When is food poisoning most likely to occur?
22 What should you do if you are given dirty china or cutlery in a café?

Kitchen Safety

1   If electrical appliances in the kitchen are to be safe what precautions must be taken?

2   What is the rule about small children and electric equipment which is working?

3   Is it safe to fill a plugged-in kettle with water even if the switch is at "off"?

4   Is it all right to wash hand mixers whilst they are plugged in, even if the switch is at "off"?

5   Before ironing what safety checks should you make?

6   If the coins for the gas meter run out what should you do for safety's sake?

7   If you have automatic taps on your gas cooker what must you always make sure of?

8   If the oven has a drop-down door what extra care must be taken if there are small children about?

9   What must you always do before cleaning an electric cooker?

10   Cloths and curtains often cause fires when they are near cookers. How can these accidents be avoided?

11   What are the main safety rules for frying?

12   What is the safest floor covering for the kitchen?

13   How can you prevent accidents with knives and other sharp objects in the kitchen?

14   What would you do to prevent accidents from cleaning liquids in the kitchen?

15   Good ventilation prevents accidents. How can kitchens be well ventilated?

16   Working in the dark causes accidents. How would you make sure there is plenty of light in the kitchen?

17   If extra heat is needed in the kitchen, what would be the best method of getting it?

18   How can accidents involving water in the kitchen be avoided?

19   In case of accident what things should be in or near the kitchen?

Laundry

1   What are the main ways of getting the washing done?

2   How would you prepare the clothes before doing a family wash?

3   Why are clothes steeped or soaked?
4   Which things really need boiling?
5   Which materials are usually starched?
6   What are the advantages of drying clothes out of doors?
7   Suggest some methods of drying clothes indoors.
8   Why are clothes usually aired?
9   What are the usual methods of airing clothes?
10 How should household linen be stored?
11 Describe how blankets can be washed before being stored away for the summer.
12 What is the correct way to keep nappies clean and fresh?
13 What is the best way to launder bras and girdles?
14 Give the general rules for removing stains.
15 Make a list of safety rules you should observe when removing stains.
16 How would you test a piece of material to see if the colour is fast?
17 What are the main types of washing machines?
18 Describe briefly the care of a washing machine after use.
19 How would you choose an iron?
20 How should you care for your iron?
    For each of the following materials write brief notes on:
    (a) Properties.
    (b) Laundering.
21 Cotton.
22 Linen.
23 Wool.
24 Silk.
25 Rayon.
26 Nylon.
27 Terylene.
28 Lycra.
29 Flame-resistant fabrics.
30 Fibreglass.
31 How would you launder a mixture fabric?

Money

1   What does PAYE stand for?
2   What is the main Income Tax allowance?
3   Name some other usual allowances.
4   How is National Insurance usually paid?

5 Make a list of the cash benefits of National Insurance.
6 What are the main ways of saving, apart from taking out insurances?
7 Why are insurances a good thing?
8 Name some kinds of insurance apart from National Insurance.
9 In what ways could insurance be useful when you go on holiday?
10 How can the family income be used to the best advantage?
11 What precautions should you take when insuring the house and contents?
12 What is the money we pay in General Rates used for?
13 List the main ways of buying things.
14 Which are the main ways of paying for things?
15 What are the advantages of H.P.?
16 What are the disadvantages of H.P.?
17 Where can you borrow the money to buy a house?
18 How are shoppers protected?
19 What are the main points you should look for in a guarantee?
20 Make a list of the general rules for buying equipment.

Answers

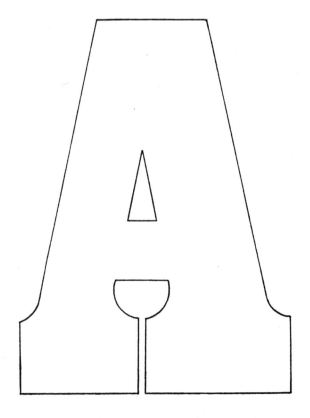

NUTRITION

General

1 Yes.

2 Growth and repair.
Energy (work and warmth).
To protect and to regulate the body processes.

3 Carbohydrates   Proteins
  Fats   Mineral elements
  Vitamins

Energy

1 For the following—
The processes of living (Basal Metabolism)—breathing,
beating of the heart, circulation of the blood, digestion of
food, to maintain body temperature.
Everyday activity—moving about, standing, sitting still,
etc.
Everyday job, e.g. office work, housework, factory work,
shop work, etc.

2 In heat units called KILOCALORIES, or megajoules (MJ).

3 "The amount of heat required to raise the temperature of one
kilogramme of water one degree Centigrade."

4 Yes.

5 Men—70 kilocalories per hour.
Women—60 kilocalories per hour.

6 Sex.   Work.
  Size.   State of health.
  Age.

7 Man—moderately active   — 3000 kilocalories.
  Woman—moderately active — 2500 kilocalories.
  Girl—13–15   — 2750 kilocalories.
  Girl—16–20   — 2500 kilocalories.
  Boy—13–15   — 3150 kilocalories.
  Boy—16–20   — 3400 kilocalories.

8 The body stores the extra food as body fat.
  The body gets fat.

9 By cutting down the kilocalorie value of their food but keeping up usual activity.
  By increasing their activity without increasing the kilocalorie value of their food.

10 (a) 1 gramme of carbohydrate gives 4 kilocalories
    (b) 1 gramme of fat gives 9 kilocalories
    (c) 1 gramme of protein gives 4 kilocalories

Carbohydrates

1 Carbon, hydrogen and oxygen.

2 Sugars, starch and cellulose.

3 Single sugars—monosaccharides.
  Double sugars—disaccharides.

4 Single—Glucose—Found in—Blood of living animals.
                        Fruit and plant juices.
                        Honey.
    Fructose—Found in—Fruit and plant juices.
                    Honey.
    Galactose—Not found free. Part of Lactose.
  Double—Sucrose—Found in—Cane and beet sugars.
                      Fruits, carrots.
    Lactose—Found in—Milk.
    Maltose—Formed from starch when barley grain germinates.

5 Cane and beet sugar, honey, jam, syrup, dried fruit.

6 It is a polysaccharide.
  Made up of many glucose molecules.

It is not sweet.
Will not dissolve in cold water.
Plants store their food supply as starch.

7   Cereals—e.g. wheat, oats, barley.
Food made with cereals—e.g. cakes and puddings.
Potatoes.
Pulses.

8   No, it must be cooked.

9   It is the only carbohydrate from animals.
The body makes it from glucose.
It is stored in the liver and muscles.
It is changed back into glucose when the body needs it.

10   It is a complicated carbohydrate.
It is formed as the intermediate stage when the body digests
starch into glucose.
It is formed when starch is heated.
It is more digestible than starch.

11   It is a complex carbohydrate.
Has no food value for human beings.
It is found in just ripe fruit and may be developed in under-
ripe fruit.
Forms a jelly which causes jam to set. (See also Preservation).

12   It is a complicated carbohydrate.
Forms the framework of plants.
Can be softened by cooking.
The human body cannot use cellulose for food but it is very
useful as roughage.

13   Vegetables, fruits, wholemeal bread, oatmeal and nuts.

14   Dry heat—Sugar melts, then caramelises and then burns.
Wet heat—Sugar dissolves and becomes syrupy. Then
caramelises and burns when the water has evaporated.

15   Dry heat—Starch changes into dextrin, then burns.
Wet heat—Starch grains soften, swell and then burst.
After this the starch dissolves in the liquid and forms a paste.

16 Sugar—Complicated sugars are converted to glucose in the small intestine.
Glucose is absorbed mainly through the walls of the small intestine.
Starch is partly broken down by saliva in the mouth.
The breakdown into glucose is completed in the small intestine.
The digested carbohydrate may be—
Used for energy straight away.
Stored as glycogen in the liver. Then changed back to glucose when needed by the body for energy.
Stored in the body as fat.

17 For energy, for work and warmth.

18 Vitamin B_1. (Thiamine.)

19 The body gets too fat.

20 Sugar is sweet and is a food.
Saccharin is sweet but is not a food.

Proteins

1 Yes.

2 Carbon, hydrogen, oxygen and nitrogen.

3 Amino acids are the simple units of which proteins are made up.

4 At least 22.

5 Yes.

6 They are essential to the body.
The body cannot make them.
The body must get them from food.
There are 8 essential amino acids that the adult person needs. There are 10 essential amino acids that children need.

7 Animal protein and vegetable protein.

8 Animal protein usually contains all the essential amino acids (the animal protein gelatine doesn't).
Vegetable protein does not usually contain all the essential amino acids the body needs (soya bean flour does).

9 Yes, most people need a mixture of animal protein foods and vegetable protein foods.

10 Animal—Meat, milk, fish, eggs, cheese.
Vegetable—Cereals, pulses, nuts, vegetables.

11 For growth and repair of the body.
Any extra, the body uses for heat and other energy.

12 Yes, because they are growing fast.

13 To make the baby's body.
For milk to feed the baby.

14 Yes.

15 Unchanged in the mouth.
Partly broken down in the stomach.
Broken down into amino acids in the small intestine.
Absorbed through the walls of the small intestine.
Carried by the blood to the liver, then into the general circulation.
Used for growth or repair, or energy.

16 It coagulates (sets).

17 Shrinks and becomes hard.
Becomes indigestible.

18 No.

19 So that the protein can be used for body building.

Fat

1 For ENERGY—for work and warmth.
To form body fat.

2 A more concentrated food.

3 Yes.

4 To protect them.

5 Carbon, hydrogen, oxygen.

6 Fatty acids and glycerol.

7 (a) and (b) The fatty acids.

8 Vitamins A, D, E.

9 (a) Lard.
(b) Beef fat.
(c) Cooking oil.

10 Yes.

11 Animal and vegetable.

12 Butter, cream, cheese, egg yolk,
Fat from meat, dripping, suet, lard,
Oily fish, fish liver oils.

13 Oils and fats from nuts and seeds, e.g. almond, coconut,
corn oil, sunflower oil, olive oil, soya bean oil.

14 Often a mixture of animal and vegetable fats.
May be all vegetable fat—suitable for vegetarians.

15 The fat melts.
Any moisture evaporates.
Too much heat causes fat to get too hot. It then decomposes
into fatty acids and glycerol.

16 Unchanged in the mouth or stomach.
In the small intestine;
Emulsified by bile.
Broken down into fatty acids and glycerol.
The fat is then ready to be absorbed through the walls of
the small intestine.

17 Yes. This means that meals containing fat are satisfying and long lasting.

18 Because without carbohydrate foods the fat will not be completely burnt. This causes Ketosis (sickness).

Vitamins

1 For growing.
Bones and teeth.
Healthy sight.
Healthy skin and linings of bronchial tubes and stomach, etc.
To help resistance to disease.

2 Eyes can't see so well, sometimes become night blind.
Infection of throat, etc.
Rough and sore skin.
Bones and teeth do not form properly.

3 As Vitamin A—
In fatty parts of foods.
Fish liver oils.
Liver, kidney, egg yolk, butter, margarine (added to).
As carotene—
Carrots, spinach, watercress, tomatoes, dried apricots.
Notes:
(a) The vitamin A in dairy foods is usually higher in summer when the animals can have green grass.
(b) The body can partly change carotene into vitamin A.
Because the body can't completely change carotene into vitamin A, vitamin A is better for the body.

4 Yes. Dark green outer leaves should never be thrown away. They should be well washed and put on to cook before the rest of the greens are added.

5 Yes, the body can store vitamin A in the liver.
This means that any extra eaten one day can be used on another day when very little has been eaten.

6 Children.
Expectant and nursing mothers.
People who do not digest fat very well may need extra
vitamin A in fish liver oil capsules.

7 Vitamin A is not affected by ordinary cooking.

8 No, vitamin A will not dissolve in water.
It will dissolve in fat and is called "fat soluble".

9 There are at least 11 vitamins in this group.

10 They are all soluble in water.

11 The body cannot store them so it needs a daily supply.

12 To help the body use carbohydrate for energy.
For growth and general health.
For the health of the nervous system.

13 Yeast and yeast extracts.
Lean meat, pork, bacon, ham, liver.
Fish and fish roes, eggs.
Bread (added to most flour) and wholegrain cereals.

14 Children.
Expectant and nursing mothers.
People doing heavy work and anybody else eating a lot of
carbohydrate foods.

15 Children don't grow properly.
Loss of appetite and poor digestion.
One will feel tired and miserable.
May begin to get disease called beriberi (not often in
England).

16 Not affected by ordinary cooking, although it will dissolve
into the cooking water.
More is lost at very high temperatures, e.g. by pressure
cooking and canning.

17 Yes, vitamin B_1 is destroyed by bicarbonate of soda.

18 Helps the body use food for energy.
Helps the body to use food fats and amino acids.
Growth.

19 Yeast and yeast products.   Milk, cheese, eggs.
Lean meat, liver, kidney.   Pulses, nuts, bread.

20 Children.
Expectant and nursing mothers.

21 Children don't grow properly.
Cracks and sores at corners of mouth, and sore tongue.
Eyes may become misty.

22 Some is lost in ordinary cooking.
More is lost at very high temperature.

23 Yes.

24 For helping it use food for energy.
Growth.

25 Yeast and yeast products.
Lean meat, liver, kidney.
Herrings and white fish.
Potatoes, whole grain cereals, bread.

26 Children.
Expectant and nursing mothers.

27 Children don't grow properly.
Skin becomes rough and red.
Diarrhoea and poor digestion.
Very little?—Mental disorder and the disease called pellagra
(not often in England).

28 Not affected by ordinary cooking but will dissolve in the
cooking water.

29 For growth.
Healing wounds and broken bones.
General health e.g. vitality, healthy teeth and skin.

30 No—therefore a daily supply is necessary.

31 Citrus fruits—oranges, lemons, grapefruit.
   Blackcurrants, strawberries, gooseberries.
   Cabbages, sprouts, new potatoes, tomatoes.
   Rose-hip syrup.
   Canned, frozen, and dried fruits and vegetables all contain
   a useful amount.

32 Babies and children.
   Expectant and nursing mothers.
   Invalids.

33 Children don't grow properly.
   Mouth and gums get sore.
   Slow healing of wounds and broken bones.
   May get a disease called scurvy.

34 Some lost in cooking.
   More lost if the food is kept hot.
   Some lost by oxidation, e.g. if vegetables are cut or bruised.

35 Yes, so people need some every day.

36 Eat fruit and vegetables raw when possible.
   Always use fresh fruit and vegetables.
   Don't let fruit and vegetables get crushed or bruised.
   Soak for as short a time as possible.
   Cook quickly—shred, and use small amount of water.
   Serve as soon as possible after cooking.
   Use cooking liquids for soups or gravies, etc.

37 For making strong bones and teeth.

38 Children's bones remain soft (rickets) and their teeth are
   poor.
   Adults' bones may become soft and teeth poor.

39 Fish liver oils.
   Oily fish, e.g. sardines, herrings, salmon.
   Dairy foods—some, but less in winter.
   Vitaminised margarine.

40 By the action of sunshine on the skin.

41 Babies and children.
Expectant and nursing mothers.

42 Not destroyed by ordinary cooking.

43 No, but it will dissolve in fat and is called "fat soluble"
(like vitamin A).

Mineral Elements

1 Elements needed by the body besides carbon, hydrogen,
oxygen and nitrogen.

2 For body building, e.g. for bones and teeth.
To make the cells of the body, e.g. muscles, nerves,
brain cells, etc.
For making body fluids, e.g. blood, sweat, digestive juices, etc.
For the normal working of the body, e.g. the clotting of
blood.

3 Calcium, phosphorus, iron, sodium, iodine.

4 To make strong bones and teeth.
To keep muscles in good working order.
To help the clotting of blood.

5 Because they are growing.
They need calcium especially to build strong bones and
teeth.

6 They don't grow properly.
They get rickets.
Their teeth are poor and badly formed.

7 To form the baby's bones and teeth.
To protect their own bones and teeth.
So that the mother's milk will be rich in calcium.

8 Their bones become poor e.g. they may get brittle and break
easily.

9 Milk and cheese.

10 Bread, green vegetables, sardines and salmon—especially if the bones are eaten.
Hard water.

11 Yes. Calcium carbonate is added to flour (by law); 14 ozs to 280 lbs of flour. This is added to all flours except true wholemeal.

12 For all the fluids of the body—makes it possible for the muscles to work properly.

13 In very hot weather.
If they work in very hot places.
After very strenuous exercise.

14 In perspiration.
In urine.

15 Get muscle cramp.
Get headaches, sickness and tiredness.

16 Salt!
Salty foods, e.g. cheese, bacon and kippers.

17 So that the thyroid gland can work properly.

18 Expectant mothers.
People who live in parts of the country where there is not enough iodine in the soil and water.

19 The thyroid gland becomes enlarged (goitre).
Babies deformed, physically and mentally.

20 Sea fish, oysters, mussels.   Water.
Watercress, onions.   Iodised salt.

21 For making haemoglobin, the substance that gives blood its red colour.
Haemoglobin is needed to carry oxygen in the blood to the body tissues so that fuel foods can be burnt to provide energy.

22 Because they are born with enough to last a few months.
Then they have to get iron from food.

23 Egg yolk, finely minced liver, and sieved green vegetables (not spinach).

24 No, you should never give babies or small children tablets or other medicines containing iron. Iron medicines can make a baby very ill unless ordered by the doctor.
If adults think they need extra iron it is better if they ask the doctor first also.

25 Expectant and nursing mothers.
Girls and women during the years they are losing blood in monthly periods.

26 Yes, because it is always being lost during the general wear and tear of the body and if bleeding occurs.

27 People may tire easily. May faint sometimes.
Girls and women, especially, may get anaemia.

28 Liver, kidney, meat, corned beef, egg yolk.
Bread, dried fruit, black treacle, watercress.

29 Yes. (a) Water used for drinking and cooking.
(b) Steel knives and iron pans where these are used.

30 No. The body cannot use it because it is in an insoluble form.

31 To make strong bones and teeth (it combines with calcium).
Enables the body to get energy from food.
To keep the composition of the body fluids constant.
For making body cells everywhere.

32 Not as a rule.
Found in most foods.
Especially in milk, cheese, liver, kidney, milk, bread.

33 For muscle and blood cells.

34 Meat, fish, milk, eggs, cheese.

35 Not as a rule.

36 For healthy teeth and bones.

37 Some drinking water, fish.

38 For all body fluids.
Digestion of food.
To help regulate body temperature.
To remove waste matter.
For lubricating joints and membranes.

39 Through the:
Lungs—breathing out.
Skin—perspiration.
Kidneys—urine.
Bowels—faeces.

40 Water and drinks made with or containing water.
Food.
Oxidation of energy foods.

41 About 2½ pints of liquid (or 1 litre).

Meal Planning

1 The age, sex, and state of health of each member of the family.
What work they do.
Their likes and dislikes, within reason.

2 No, they must have a balanced diet.

3 A balanced diet is one which contains enough of all the nutrients.

4 The number of people.
How much money is available.
The amount of time there is to prepare, cook and eat the food.
The season of the year.
The time of day.
What shopping and storage facilities there are.
The capability of the cook.

Whether the meal is an everyday family meal or a special occasion meal.

How far ahead the meals can be planned, e.g. a whole day's meals or the meals for a week.

5 By using different foods.
Having a variety of flavours.
Using differently textured foods.
By not using food of all one colour, e.g. all white foods.
Serving everything attractively.
Cooking the foods by different methods.

6 No, the protein food should be divided between the day's meals.

7 Protein first.
Protective foods next.
Energy foods last.

8 Yes, because it contains all the nutrients that a baby needs.

9 Orange juice, rose hip syrup, blackcurrant purée.

10 Cod liver oil and halibut liver oil.

11 Egg yolk, minced liver and sieved green vegetables (not spinach).

12 Yes, it is very important that children of all ages always have enough of the protective foods. They always need plenty of fruit, vegetables and dairy foods.

13 Protein, because it is the main nutrient for the growth and repair of the body.

14 Carbohydrate, because it is the main energy food, but they also need some energy-giving fat because it is less bulky.

15 It is very important for children of all ages to have a well-balanced diet so that their bodies can grow properly and the children can be healthy in every way.

16 Apples, carrots, rusks and other crispy foods.

c

17 About $1\frac{1}{2}$ to 2 pints (or $\frac{3}{4}$ to 1 litre).
This may be drunk or made into puddings, etc.

18 Yes. This is particularly important where the protective and protein foods are concerned.

19 No, because they can neither eat enough food, nor can the food they eat be properly digested if they are overtired.

20 Yes, but mealtimes should still be pleasant occasions for small children.

21 No, they should have plenty of time to eat their meals. If they are hurried too often they lose their appetite and are likely to leave important foods.

22 Yes, they should have any cutlery or "china" which makes it easy for them to eat their food. When they are older they can soon learn to use what everybody else uses.

23 Yes, and then they can be given more if they want it. Small children are sometimes put off by large amounts of food.

24 Regularity of meals is a good general rule, and is worth keeping.
If small children have to wait too long for their food they sometimes lose their desire for food. They also eat things which they should not eat, and this is sometimes dangerous.

25 No, because they soon want "sauce" on everything. This can be bad for their digestion as well as stopping them being interested in new foods and flavours.

26 No, because sweets take away the child's appetite for the more important foods.
If a child is to be allowed to eat sweets, one or two after a meal is best.

27 Yes. The food should be as varied as possible and not consist almost entirely of biscuits and sweetstuffs.

28 All young people need food for growing because their bodies are growing until they are at least 20.

29 Yes, they should still have milk. The milk may be in various forms and served in various ways.

30 Most teenagers do use up a great déal of energy and need energy foods for this. As for younger children, some of this energy food may be carbohydrate and some needs to be less bulky fat. However, it is important that teenagers should not get into the habit of overeating just because people are always making remarks about their big appetites.

31 To enable their bodies to make the most of the carbohydrate foods they eat teenagers need plenty of vitamin B_1.

32 Teenage girls should eat plenty of foods containing iron to prevent them becoming anaemic. If necessary, they should go to the doctor for advice.

33 Yes, because as soon as they start work they usually have to choose at least their mid-day meal themselves.

34 A well-balanced diet.
Any particular orders of the doctor.
Welfare foods such as milk, vitamin tablets, iron tablets, etc.
If digestion is poor it may be as well to avoid a lot of fried foods.

35 For the health of the mother.
To make the baby's body grow.

36 To keep up their own store of iron.
To supply the baby with iron.

37 To protect the mother's bones and teeth.
To make the baby's bones and teeth.

38 For her own general health.
For the general health of the baby. To build up its resistance to disease and to make strong bones and teeth.

39 Milk—about 2 pints a day (or 1 litre).
Meat, fish or cheese—every day.
Green vegetables—twice a day.
Root vegetables—twice a day.

Vitamin C fruits—every day.
Eggs—one a day.
Liver—2 or 3 times a week.
Vitamin and mineral tablets as ordered by the doctor.
Enough carbohydrate foods to keep off sickness but not
enough to make the body overweight.

40 From the very beginning of her pregnancy.

41 Yes, for her own and the baby's health.

42 She would have to take continuous care of her diet for her
babies' health and so that her own health would be kept at
a high level.

43 Not too much carbohydrate food.
Plenty of fruit and vegetables.
Small meals at shorter intervals better than fewer large
meals each day.
Food should be easily digested.

44 Yes. They need a well-balanced diet the same as the rest of
the family.
Regular meals are better than biscuit and tea snacks.

45 They need meals which contain plenty of carbohydrates and
vitamin B_1. Some of the extra kilocalories they need should
be in the form of less bulky fat.
They also need the correct amount of protein foods and
protective foods.

46 Steak and kidney puddings, fried fish and chips, meat and
fruit pies as well as sandwiches and pulse vegetables.

47 Because it is less bulky than carbohydrate foods.

48 Yes, although they may not need as much energy food as
they used to.

49 (a) Their bones become poor.
(b) All milk dishes and any cheese dishes they can eat.

50 Their teeth should be seen to.

They should have food they can easily digest.
They must always have a diet which contains enough of all
the nutrients.

51 Yes. At least they should have an orange or tomatoes, 2 or 3
times a week. If this is not possible they may have to have
vitamin C in tablet form. It is better if a doctor is consulted.

52 Yes, but they often cannot afford to buy protein foods.
"Meals on wheels" services will provide meals for old
people who cannot go shopping, prepare or afford proper
food.

53 White fish, eggs, minced lean meat, chicken. Pork should
be avoided.

54 Strict vegetarians—They do not eat any animal food.
Lacto-vegetarians—They do not eat meat, poultry or fish.
 They will eat milk, eggs and cheese.

55 To supply the essential amino acids.
To supply vitamins A and D.
To supply enough calcium, iron and phosphorus.
To plan meals that are not bulky and hard to digest.
Vegetarian foods are often dear.

56 Pulses, cereals, nuts and root vegetables.
Vegetable oils, nut oils, margarine.
Green vegetables.
Vegetable extracts, spices and herbs.

57 Health food shops.
Some chemists.
Cookery books.
Clinics in the case of children.
Some doctors.

58 To consult their doctor.

59 Increase protein foods.
Eat plenty of protective foods.
Cut down on carbohydrate-rich foods.
Check up with the doctor if there is any loss of energy or
well-being.

60 Yes, it does. They should be as well balanced as possible in relation to the rest of the day's meals.

61 Useful foods include:
Cold meat, hard-boiled eggs, tinned fish, cheese.
Salad vegetables, fruit—fresh and dried.
Meat pies, sausage rolls, fruit pies, fruit cake, etc.

62 They should contain some moist food (but not soggy sandwiches).
They should be packed neatly.
A suitable drink should be included.
All the food should be convenient to eat.

63 Obey the doctor's orders.

64 If possible the food should be prepared and served out of sight and sound of the sick room.
The meals should be served regularly and on time (unless the doctor says don't wake the patient for meals).
The food and everything else on the tray should look attractive.

65 Yes, the method of cooking food for invalids is very important. They should not be given fried foods.
Steaming and grilling are usually the most useful methods.

66 Liquids only, e.g. milk drinks, fruit juices, barley water, jellies, drinks made of meat and vegetable extracts.

67 White fish, steamed or grilled.
Egg dishes, e.g. custards; eggs poached, scrambled, lightly boiled.
Milk and milk dishes, e.g. junkets, moulds, milk jellies, etc.
Vitamin C fruit and fruit drinks.

68 Body building foods—white fish, lean meat, poultry, eggs.
Protective foods—Vitamin C fruit, vegetables.
Milk drinks and fruit drinks.

69 Pork, fried foods, suet puddings, oily fish, shellfish, foods the patient really doesn't like.

70 Plan the meals for as many days ahead as possible.
Check the refrigerator and the larder so that you only buy
the food you need.
Make a list.

71 Only if the family like that particular food.
Only if you have plenty of storage space.
Only if you are sure the food is in good condition.

72 Yes, because it can save time for the busy housewife.
She should however make a point of visiting the shops
sometimes to check up on the prices.

73 (a) Meat with bone—6 ozs (150 g).
Meat without bone—4 ozs (100 g).

(b) Fish with bone—6 ozs (150 g).
Fish without bone—4 ozs (100 g).

74 Potatoes—6 ozs (150 g).
Greens—6 ozs (150 g).
Root vegetables—6 ozs (150 g).
Fresh peas and runner beans—6 ozs (150 g).
Fruit for stewing—4 ozs (100 g).

75 Flour for puddings and pies—1½ ozs (40 g).
Milk for custard and milk puddings ¼ pint (125 ml).
Soup ½ pint (250 ml).

FOOD

Methods of Cooking

1   To make it safe to eat—harmful bacteria killed.
    To make it digestible.
    To make it attractive to look at and taste.

2   Boiling, stewing, steaming, braising.
    Grilling, baking, roasting, frying.

3   Long, slow moist method. Liquid just simmers.
    In pan on top of stove (lid on).
    In casserole in oven.

4   Cheap cuts of meat may be used.
    Little loss of nutrients.
    Little fuel used.
    Doesn't need much attention.

5   Cheap cuts of meat, fresh or dried fruit.

6   Moist method.
    Food is cooked in steam rising from boiling water.
    Direct contact—food is cooked in a steamer or in a basin
    in a pan of boiling water.
    Indirect contact—food is cooked between 2 plates over a
    pan of boiling water.
    Food may be wrapped in greaseproof paper, or foil,
    unwrapped, or in a basin.

7   Food more digestible.
    Little loss of nutrients.
    Puddings lighter.
    Food not broken.
    Economical on fuel with careful planning.

8   Puddings, fish, custards, potatoes, marrow, root vegetables.

9   Water must be kept boiling.
    Well-fitting lid to prevent steam escaping.
    Water in pan must be boiling before food is put in steamer, etc.

10 Cooking by steam under high pressure.
High temperature.

11 Short time.
Economical on fuel.

12 Nowadays it usually means food cooked in the oven in fat.
If the food is cooked in an open tin the fat is usually
spooned over it every now and again to prevent the outside
getting hard and dry.
If the food is cooked in a closed tin or wrapped in foil
basting may not be necessary.

13 Tender and fairly tender cuts of meat, root vegetables,
potatoes.

14 Moist method.
Combination of stewing and roasting.
Food cooked on a bed of vegetables—called a 'Mirepoix'.
Stock is added to come half way up the sides of the meat.
Cooking done on top of the cooker and then in the oven
or all in the oven.
Lid must be tight fitting—removed about $\frac{1}{2}$ hour before
cooking is finished.

15 Tough meat, or poultry. Vegetables.

16 Quick method using radiant heat.
Outside of food seals quickly—flavour kept.

17 Meat, fish, chicken joints, tomatoes, mushrooms, toast,
savouries on toast.

18 Foods rich in fat may be fried with no extra fat, e.g.
bacon.
Little fat used for eggs, pancakes.
Little more for liver and lean steak.
Fat halfway up sides of food for fishcakes, rissoles, thick fish.

19 Food covered by fat.
Fat pan half full of fat.
Must use deep heavy pan.
Frying basket necessary for some foods.
Most food is coated.

20 Cutlets, fish, doughnuts, fritters, chips.

21 Seasoned flour.   Batter.
     Flour, egg and breadcrumbs.   Pastry.

22 Cooking fats.
     Frying oils.
     Lard.
     Butter and olive oil sometimes used.

23 Clean fat at the correct temperature.
     Deep fat frying—don't put too much food in the pan.
     Never drop food into the fat.
     Drain food on absorbent paper.
     Strain fat after use.

Meat

1 Bullock—beef.
   Sheep—lamb and mutton.
   Pig—pork.
   Rabbit.
   Domestic birds—chickens, turkeys, geese, ducks.
   Game birds—pheasant, partridge, grouse.

2 Muscle tissue consisting of bundles of fibre held together by connective tissue.

3 The meat from old animals. The fibres are thick and long.

4 The parts where the muscles are used most, e.g., chicken-leg, beef-shin.

5 The hard protective fat round the internal organs of animals. The suet round ox kidneys is usually used in cooking.

6 Good colour, lean and fat.
   Fresh smell.
   Flesh firm and elastic to touch.
   Moist but not wet.
   Fine even grain.
   Not too much bone.

7 Animal protein.
Fat.
Vitamins—mainly B group. Some A.
Mineral salts—some sulphur, phosphorus, iron.
Water.

8 They are substances which:
Give meat its flavour.
Help digestion.
Have no food value.

9 To kill bacteria.
To make it tender and digestible.
To make it look and taste better.
To develop extractives, for flavour.

10 Roasting, grilling, frying, boiling, stewing, braising.

11 Sirloin, top rump, rib, aitchbone.

12 Shoulder, leg, best end of neck, breast.

13 Leg, loin, fillet, blade, spare rib.

14 Loin, fillet, breast.

15 Beef—15 minutes to the pound + 20 minutes.
Lamb—20 minutes to the pound + 20 minutes.
Pork—25 minutes to the pound + 25 minutes.
Veal—25 minutes to the pound + 25 minutes.
These times are approximate. 1 lb may be taken as $\frac{1}{2}$ kilo.

16 Yes, they do.

17 The protein hardens. This makes the meat indigestible.

18 Small tender cuts, e.g. fillet and rump steaks, chops, cutlets, kidneys.

19 Beef—topside, silverside, brisket, ox tongue.
Pork—ham, cheek, belly (pickled).
Mutton—leg, middle neck.

20 Stewing is suitable for cheap cuts of meat, e.g.:
Beef—shin, neck, thin flank, chuck steak.
Lamb or mutton—middle neck, scrag end of neck.
Veal—breast, neck, knuckle.

21 Most tougher cuts of meat not suitable for roasting.

22 Liver, heart, kidney, brain, tongue, sweetbreads, tripe.

23 Liver—fry, stew, braise, make into patés.
Kidney—fry, grill, stew, pies, soup.
Heart—roast, stew, braise.
Tripe—stew.
Sweetbreads—fry, grill, steam, stew.

24 Animal protein.
Iron in liver and kidney.
Vitamin A, especially in liver.
Vitamin B group.

25 Plump breast, smooth legs, fresh smell, not discoloured.

26 Protein—animal.   Iron.
Vitamin B group.   Phosphorus.

27 Roasting, boiling, casserole, frying, grilling.

28 Beef—yorkshire pudding, horseradish sauce, mustard, thin gravy.
Lamb—mint sauce, thin gravy (thick if the joint is stuffed).
Mutton—onion sauce, redcurrant jelly, thin gravy (thick if joint stuffed).
Pork—apple sauce, sage and onion stuffing, thick gravy.
Veal—bacon rolls, lemon slices, veal forcemeat stuffing, thick gravy.
Chicken—bread sauce, veal forcemeat, bacon rolls, thin gravy.

29 Salt beef—carrot, turnip, onion, dumplings, gravy (strained cooking liquor used).
Mutton—same vegetables as for salt beef. Caper sauce.

30 Grilled tomatoes, mushrooms, fried potatoes, parsley butter.

31 The vegetables that were cooked with the meat may be used. Also separate vegetables such as carrots and swede.

32 The vegetables that were cooked with the meat. Also separate vegetables. Mashed potatoes or plain boiled potatoes. The cooking liquor may be served as it is, or thickened.

Fish

1 White, oily, shell.

2 Yes, it is stored in the liver (there is very little in the flesh).

3 Cod, whiting, haddock, sole, halibut.

4 Herrings, mackerel, salmon, eel, pilchards.

5 Shrimps, crab, lobster, oysters, cockles.

6 White—easily digested.
Oily—less easy to digest because of the fat.
Shell—difficult to digest because the flesh fibres are tough.

7 Protein—is animal.
Fat—oily fish has fat in flesh.
  white fish, mainly in liver.
Calcium ⎫
Phosphorus ⎬ good source if bones are eaten.
Vitamins A and D—in fat.
  B group—some.
Water.

8 No unpleasant smell.   Bright eyes and gills.
Flesh firm and moist.   Plenty of scales.

9 Frying—conserves flavour and nutritive value.
Steaming—for small pieces.
Grilling—conserves flavour and nutritive value.
Boiling—suitable for large fish.
Baking—conserves flavour. Baked fish may be stuffed.
Sousing (cooking in vinegar), e.g. herrings.

10 Garnishes, e.g. lemon, watercress, tomatoes, chopped eggs, grapes.
Sauces, e.g. Parsley, cheese, tartare.

Milk

1   Cow's milk mostly but milk from goats is sometimes used.

2   Animal protein.
Fat.
Carbohydrate—milk sugar (lactose).
Vitamins—A (more in summer), B group, D (small amount),
Minerals—rich in calcium and phosphorus.

3   Cows are kept in hygienic conditions.
Milk is transported as quickly as possible and in hygienic conditions.
There are special hygiene rules for milk handlers.
Milk may be tested at any stage.
Milk is processed to destroy any harmful bacteria.

4   Never leave milk outside (loss of vitamin A and riboflavine).
Keep cool and covered—in refrigerator if possible.
Always use clean jugs.
Never mix old and new milk.
Don't leave milk near strong smelling food or any other strong smelling substances.
To keep milk, boil it or scald it.

5   Untreated, Pasteurised, Sterilised, Ultra heat treated, Homogenised. Channel Islands and South Devon.

6   Different kinds of cream.
Butter.
Condensed milk—evaporated with sugar added.
Evaporated milk—water reduced.
Dried milk, full cream and skimmed.
Cheese.
Yoghourt.

7   Protein is animal.
The fat is easily digested.

Rich in calcium.
Well digested by most people, especially if added to cereals.
Not easily tired of.

8 Very little iron.
Low in vitamin C, and some of the B group and D.
Poor in carbohydrate.
No roughage for adults.
May carry disease.

9 Milk drinks.
Added to cereals.
In puddings, moulds, jellies, junket, custard, soups, sauces,
cakes, etc.

Cheese

1 Milk is clotted with rennet or acid, or is soured by bacteria.
Whey is strained from the curd.
The curd is melted and pressed.
The curd is left to ripen. The flavour develops by the action
of bacteria and moulds.

2 Hard—e.g. Cheddar, Parmesan.
Soft—e.g. Stilton, Camembert.
Cream cheeses—have a mild flavour. They do not keep long.
Processed—cheese is ground to powder, melted with
pasteurised milk, solidified, wrapped in foil.

3 $\frac{1}{3}$ protein, $\frac{1}{3}$ fat, $\frac{1}{3}$ water.
Calcium.
Phosphorus.
Vitamins A, D, and riboflavine.

4 Grate or chop finely.
Do not overcook.
Serve with starchy foods, e.g. bread, potatoes.
Season well.

5 Grilling.
Baking in pies, flans, soufflés, cheese pastry.
Frying—cheese aigrettes.

6   As the main course of a meal, e.g. cheese pudding.
To finish a meal, e.g. cheese and biscuits.
To flavour sauce, e.g. in macaroni cheese, cheese sauce
for cauliflower, etc.
In sandwiches and rolls.

Eggs

1   Usually hen's eggs. Duck, goose and turkey eggs are also
used.

2   The average egg weighs about 2 ozs (or 50 g).
Shell—Consists of chalk
          Is porous (air and bacteria can enter, water can
          escape).
Yolk—Food store for the chicken.
          Richer than the white.
          Easily digested.
White—Good food value.
          No fat.
          Easily digested.

3   The shell should be slightly rough.
When light is passed through, the egg should appear
slightly transparent.
Should feel heavy.
Brine test: 50g salt to $\frac{1}{2}$ litre water.
                  Fresh eggs sink.
                  Stale eggs rise.

4   As a main dish—instead of meat or fish.
Thickening, e.g. sauces.
Binding, e.g. fish cakes.
Coating, e.g. Scotch eggs.
Enriching, e.g. milk puddings.
Lightening, e.g. meringues, cakes.
Emulsifier, e.g. mayonnaise.
Glaze—for pastry.
Garnish, e.g. for crab.

5   Boiling, frying, poaching, baking, steaming.

6 Must be cooked for at least 10 minutes.
Should come from a reliable source.

7 Protein—animal.
Fat—in yolk.
Mineral elements—iron, calcium and some phosphorus.
Vitamins—A, D and some B group.

Cereals

1 The seeds of cultivated grasses, e.g. wheat, oats, barley, rye, rice, and maize.

2 A rich source of carbohydrate.
Useful amounts of vegetable protein.
Small amounts of fat.
Good source of vitamin B group but some is lost in milling.

3 Wheat.

4 Made from the endosperm of hard wheat; takes the form of hard little grains. Used for puddings, thickening soups and sometimes in biscuits.

5 Made from hard wheat.
Made into a paste with water, and sometimes eggs.
Drawn into tubes or moulded into shapes, e.g. macaroni, spaghetti, noodles.

6 A protein.
It can absorb water to make an elastic substance.
This elastic substance stretches and holds expanded gas when cooked.

7 Sometimes made into oatmeal. Sold fine, medium and ground.
Also rolled to make "rolled oats" for porridge.
Food value—useful amounts of protein, fat, carbohydrate and vitamin B group.

8 Sold as pearl barley.
Used for barley water and for thickening soups.

9 The rice used in this country is usually sold polished.
Used for milk puddings and savoury dishes.
Ground rice is used for cakes.
Food value—mainly starch, poor in protein, fat and mineral
elements.

10 Called "Corn" sometimes.
Cornflour is made from maize. Used for making blancmange,
and for thickening sauces, soups, and stews.
Sweet corn, or corn on the cob, is used as a vegetable.

11 They are not true cereals.
They are nearly 100% starch.
Arrowroot comes from the maranta plant. It is used for
puddings and for thickening.
Sago comes from the sago palm. It is used for milk puddings.
Tapioca comes from the cassava plant. It is used for milk
puddings.

Fats

1 For making cakes, pastry, puddings, etc.
Frying.
To add flavour and food value.
For making sauces and soups.
For basting meat during cooking.
To grease baking tins.

2 Butter is made by churning separated cream.
It contains about 85% of fat.
Butyric acid gives butter its pleasant taste and smell.
Butter contains vitamins A and D—more in the summer
months.
It is used for—
Spreading on bread.
Making cakes, pastry, biscuits, etc.
Cream for filling cakes.
Sauces.

3 Lard is a soft white fat which comes from the pig.
It is 100% fat.
It has a low melting point.

Lard contains none of the vitamins A and D.
It is used for making pastry (usually with margarine) and
for frying.

4   Suet is a hard fat which comes from round the kidneys of
animals, e.g. ox and sheep.
It is usually sold shredded nowadays.
It is used for making suet pastry and puddings.

5   Dripping is the fat which has dripped from meat.
It has the flavour of the kind of meat it has come from.
It contains water and so is likely to go rancid.
Dripping needs to be clarified before being used for cooking
purposes.
Clarified dripping can be used for making pastry or for
frying.

6   Olive oil is not usually used for cooking in this country,
although it can be used for some shallow frying.
It is usually used for making salad dressing.

7   Frying and cooking oils.
Some are just for frying, but some can also be used for
cake making, etc.
They do not contain any water.
They have a high smoking point.

8   Cooking fats are usually white fats.
Some are ready creamed.
They are used for making cakes and pastry as well as for
frying.

9   Margarine may be made from animal and vegetable fats or
just vegetable fats, e.g. for vegetarians.
Vitamins A and D must be added to margarine (by law).
There are several different types of margarine available,
e.g. soft for caking making and table use, harder for pastry
making, fat-reduced for slimmers.
Margarine may be used in most recipes using fat, e.g. cakes,
pastry, puddings, biscuits, etc.

Vegetables

1   For essential vitamins and minerals.
    For roughage.
    For their flavour and colour.

2   Vegetable protein—some (most in pulses).
    Carbohydrates—Starch—potatoes.
                   Sugar—beetroot, onions, tomatoes.
                   Starch and Sugar—peas, broad beans, pulses.
    Mineral elements—some calcium and iron but the body
                   cannot always digest it.
    Vitamins—A—as Carotene; carrots and green vegetables
             are rich sources.
             B-group—A little in most vegetables.
             Pulses a rich source.
             C—rich sources are green vegetables, tomatoes
             new potatoes. Some in most vegetables.

3   Sprouts, cabbage, cauliflowers, spinach, water-cress, curly
    kale, turnip tops.

4   Vitamin A in vegetables is in the form of Carotene. Dark
    green leafy vegetables contain most Carotene. Carrots are
    rich in vitamin A in the form of Carotene.

5   Yes, because they contain more vitamins and minerals than
    cooked vegetables.

6   Some vitamin C is lost.
    Starch grains are ruptured.
    Become more digestible.

7   Green—good colour, firm, crisp, medium size.
    Root—firm, free from soil, no sprouting, no spade marks.
    Freshly picked vegetables are best.

8   Peel thinly with a sharp knife.
    Prepare just before cooking.
    Don't soak too long.
    Bicarbonate of soda destroys vitamin B1, don't use it too
    often.

Use dark outside leaves—cook them about 5 minutes
before adding the rest.
Cook for the shortest time.

9 Boiling, baking, roasting, grilling, frying, braising, stewing,
the conservative method.

10 (a) Toss in butter—peas, carrots, potatoes.
   (b) Serve with a sauce—cauliflower, beetroot, marrow.
   (c) Sprinkle with chopped parsley—potatoes, carrots.

11 Peas, beans, lentils.

12 Soak all night.
Rinse.
Cook until tender (some people add a very little bicarbonate
of soda although this destroys vitamin B_1).

13 Canning, drying, freezing.

14 Chicory, sweet peppers, globe artichokes, aubergines.

15 Don't prepare too far in advance.
Don't leave prepared salads in a warm place.
All ingredients must be very clean.
Don't handle ingredients more than necessary.

16 French dressing, salad cream, mayonnaise, vinaigrette.

Fruit

1 Some fruits are rich in vitamin C.
Some fruits supply vitamin A.
It is refreshing.
It is useful served with, or cooked with other foods.

2 *Very good sources*   *Good sources*
   Rose hips   Oranges
   Blackcurrants   Lemons
   Redcurrants   Grapefruit
   Strawberries   Raspberries
                                Gooseberries
                                Loganberries.

3   Apricots, tomatoes, peaches.

4   Makes some fruit easier to digest.
Destroys some bacteria.
Destroys some vitamin C.

5   Stewing—most fruits.
Baking—apples.
Cooked in baked pies, steamed puddings.
Making into fruit drinks.

6   Canning, freezing, drying, crystallising, bottling.

Stock

1   Stock is the liquid in which meat bones and vegetables, or fish bones and vegetables, have been simmered for a long time.

2   Stock contains little food value but it stimulates the appetite.

3   Well flavoured.
Free from grease.
The right colour, e.g. white for white soups and sauces.

4   Cooked and raw meat and bones.
Bones and trimmings of white fish for fish stock.
The liquor in which the meat or fish has been cooked.
Vegetables and their trimmings.
Water.

5   Starchy foods, e.g. potatoes and bread. They make the stock sour. Green vegetables and the water they have been cooked in. They give the stock a bitter flavour.
Turnips.
Salty liquor, e.g. from salt meat.
Food which has begun to go bad.

6   Brown, white and fish.

7 Fresh clean ingredients.
Strong deep pan with a well-fitting lid.
Meat cut small, vegetables rough chopped.
Balanced proportion of ingredients.
Scum removed every time it comes to the top.
Never leave stock in the pan overnight.
If stock is kept more than one day it must be heated up
every day. Bring to the boil quickly and keep boiling for
15 minutes.

8 Use suitable vegetable water + meat or yeast extracts or
meat or stock cubes.

Soup

1 It stimulates the digestive juices.
Is warming in cold weather.
Is useful for invalids.

2 Broths—chicken, scotch, mutton.
Purées—potato, pea, lentil, celery, tomato.
Clear soups—Consommés.
Cream soups—thickened.
Fish soups—bisques.

3 Meat, vegetables, cereals sometimes, e.g. pearl barley.

4 Vegetables usually sieved before serving.
Thickened with flour or cornflour—potato and lentil soups
may not need thickening.
Milk or cream sometimes added before serving.

5 Free from grease.
Good colour and flavour.
Correct consistency.

6 (a) Croûtons.
(b) Grated cheese.

Sauces

1 A sauce is a well-flavoured liquid, usually thickened.

2 They are used in a meal to:
    Add flavour.
    Add colour.
    Improve appearance and texture.
    Bind food together, e.g. rissoles.
    Add nutritive value.
    Counteract the richness of some foods, e.g. apple sauce with pork.

3 It should:
    Be well flavoured.
    Be suitable for the dish it is to be served with.
    Be made of ingredients which blend well together.
    Have a distinctive flavour.
    Be smooth and glossy.
    Be well cooked.
    Have a good colour.

4 Roux sauces, white or brown.
    Blended.
    Cooked egg sauces.
    Unclassified.

5 Equal quantities of flour and fat.

6 Pouring—$\frac{1}{2}$ oz cornflour to $\frac{1}{2}$ pint of milk (or 15 g to 250 ml).
    Coating—$\frac{3}{4}$ oz cornflour to $\frac{1}{2}$ pint milk (or 20 g to 250 ml).

7 Cheese, parsley, mustard, onion, hard-boiled egg, anchovy.

8 Flour, dripping, stock, carrots, onion, turnip, seasoning. (Mushrooms and bacon sometimes added.)

9 Custard, Hollandaise.

10 Check for consistency, colour and flavour.

11 Oil (salad or olive), egg yolk, vinegar or lemon juice, sugar, salt, pepper and mustard.

Batters

1 Plain flour, milk or water and usually egg.

2   Mainly air, also water vapour.

3   (a) Thin—1 egg, 4 ozs flour, $\frac{1}{2}$ pint milk (or 100 g flour, 250 ml milk), $\frac{1}{4}$ teaspoon salt.

   (b) Thick—1 egg, 4 ozs flour, $\frac{1}{4}$ pint milk (or 100 g flour, 125 ml milk), $\frac{1}{4}$ teaspoon salt.

4   Thin batter. Sometimes called pancake batter.

Réchauffés

1   Food which has been cooked, allowed to cool and then reheated.
The left-over food may also be made into a different dish.

2   Cool quickly.
Put into a clean, covered container.
Keep cool, in a refrigerator, if possible.

3   Make sure the food is perfectly fresh before you use it.
The food should be finely divided so that it can be heated quickly.
Protein foods should not be heated too long or the protein is hardened.
If raw ingredients are to be added, cook them first.
If extra moisture is added, e.g. gravy, make sure it is really fresh.
Never reheat food a second time.

4   Coat with breadcrumbs, e.g. rissoles and fishcakes.
Dip into batter, e.g. fritters.
Cover with potatoes, e.g. shepherd's pie.
Cover with pastry, e.g. pasties.

5   Add interesting flavours, e.g. onion, tomatoes, curry, etc.
Add vitamin C by serving vegetables and fruit which contain vitamin C.
Add garnishes, e.g. tomatoes, small pieces of toast.

6   Baking, e.g. fish pie and shepherd's pie.
Frying, e.g. fish cakes and rissoles.
Heating in a sauce, e.g. mince and curries.

7 Meat—shepherd's pie, savoury meat rolls, rissoles.
Fish—fish cakes, fish pie.
Vegetables—"Bubble and squeak", potato cakes, fish and
shepherd's pie.

Raising Agents

1 When it is cooked the mixture will be light.

2 Sieve the flour.
Rub the fat into the flour.
Cream the fat and sugar.
Beat mixtures.
Fold and roll pastry.
Add egg to mixtures.

3 By using any of the following:
Bicarbonate of soda alone.
Bicarbonate of soda plus acid.
Baking powder.
Self-raising flour.
Baking ammonia.
Yeast.

4 Yes, water vapour helps to make batters and choux pastry
rise.

5 Cream of tartar, bicarbonate of soda and rice flour.

6 Yeast is a plant.

7 Yes, yeast is alive.

8 Compressed yeast and dried yeast.

9 The yeast must have the following:
Food—flour (starch) and sugar.
Warmth.
Moisture—water or milk or a mixture of water and milk.
Time to work.

10 About 27° C.

11 Too much heat or cold.
Being kept too long.
When too much salt is used.

Bread Making

1 A strong flour, because strong flour contains plenty of good quality gluten.

2 $\frac{1}{2}$ oz of yeast for less than 1 pound of flour (or 15 g . . . $\frac{1}{2}$ kilo).
1 oz of yeast for 1 to $3\frac{1}{2}$ pounds of flour (or 25 g . . . $\frac{1}{2}$ to $1\frac{3}{4}$ kilo).
2 oz of yeast for $3\frac{1}{2}$ to 7 pounds flour (or 50 g . . . $1\frac{3}{4}$ to $3\frac{1}{2}$ kilo).

3 Creaming, sponging, mixing, kneading, rising, kneading, shaping, proving and baking.

4 Yes, the bread can be made by just doing the following steps: creaming, mixing, kneading, shaping, rising and baking.
The bread will be good to eat but not quite as light and spongy as when all the stages are completed.

5 No. Nowadays it is thought to be too drastic. Instead the yeast is creamed with a little water and then more water is whisked in.

6 Yes.

Pastry

1 Flour, fat, water.
Eggs, sugar, cheese may be used as well when making rich pastries.

2 Yes, when making:—
Suet pastry.
Shortcrust if less than $\frac{1}{2}$ fat to flour is used.

3 Air usually.
Baking powder—if less than $\frac{1}{2}$ fat to flour is used for shortcrust pastry. Also in suet pastry.
Steam in flaky and rough puff pastry.

4 (a) Suet—$\frac{1}{4}$ to $\frac{1}{2}$.
   (b) Shortcrust—$\frac{1}{2}$ and $\frac{1}{2}$.
   (c) Rough puff and flaky—$\frac{2}{3}$ to $\frac{3}{4}$.

5 (a) Suet—shredded and mixed with the flour.
   (b) Shortcrust—rubbed in to the flour.
   (c) Flaky—laid on pastry in small pats, then rolled in.
   (d) Rough puff—rough chopped, mixed with flour, then rolled in.

6 Keep everything cool.
   Use correct amount of ingredients.
   Use little flour for rolling out.
   Introduce as much air as possible.
   Handle pastry lightly.
   Leave to relax and cool.before baking.
   Use correct oven temperature.

7 "4 ozs of shortcrust pastry" means 4 ozs of flour + 2 ozs of fat (or "100 g shortcrust" means 100 g flour + 50 g fat).

8 Steaming, boiling or baking.

9 Meat and fruit puddings. Sweet or savoury roly-poly.

10 Electric 425 °F (220 °C), Gas Mark 7 until set. Then reduce to Electric 375 °F (190 °C), Gas Mark 5 until cooked.

11 Cheese pastry—Use $\frac{1}{2}$ to equal grated cheese to flour.
   Egg yolk may be used in mixing.
   Biscuit crust—Use 1 to 2 ozs caster sugar to 1 pound flour (or 25–50 g to $\frac{1}{2}$ kilo). Egg yolk may be used in mixing.

12 Savoury—meat pies, Cornish pasties, sausage rolls.
   Sweet—fruit pies, jam tarts, apple balls.

13 To give more elasticity.
   To counteract the richness.

14 To keep the air in.
   To stop the fat being squeezed out—flaky pastry.

15 To allow the pastry to relax. This prevents the pastry shrinking when it is cooked.

16 Electric 450 °F (230 °C), Gas Mark 8 until set.
Then, Electric 375 °F (190 °C), Gas Mark 5 until cooked.

17 Savoury—meat pies, vol au vents, sausage rolls.
Sweet—eccles cakes, vanilla slices, jam puffs.

Cakes

1 Flour, raising agent, fat, sugar, eggs, fruit.

2 A rich cake is made with more than $\frac{1}{2}$ fat to flour.
A plain cake is made with $\frac{1}{2}$ or less than $\frac{1}{2}$ fat to flour.

3 Plain—$\frac{1}{2}$ or less fat to flour—rubbing-in method.
Rich—more than $\frac{1}{2}$ fat to flour—creaming method.
Sponge—no fat—whisking method.
Gingerbread—melting method.

4 Rock cakes, raspberry buns, coconut cakes.
Large cakes—chocolate, coffee, etc.
Fruit loaves.

5 Small—400 °F (200 °C), Gas Mark 6.
Large—350–375 °F (180–190 °C), Gas Mark 4–5.

6 Small—chocolate, cherry, queen, etc.
Large—Victoria sandwich, rich fruit cakes, Madeira, etc.

7 Small—375 °F (190 °C), Gas Mark 5.
Large—350–375 °F (180–190 °C), Gas Mark 4–5.
Fruit—300–350 °F (150–180 °C), Gas Mark 2–4.

8 1 egg, 1 oz (25 g) caster sugar, 1 oz (25 g) plain flour

9 Small—400 °F (200 °C), Gas Mark 6.
Swiss Roll—425 °F (220 °C), Gas Mark 7
Sponge Sandwich—375 °F (190 °C), Gas Mark 5 (reduced
to 325 °F (170 °C), Gas Mark 3, if necessary).

10 Sponge drops and fingers, Swiss roll, sponge sandwich.

11 (a) $\frac{1}{3}$ to $\frac{1}{2}$ fat and sugar to plain flour.

(b) $\frac{1}{3}$ to $\frac{3}{4}$ syrup to flour.

(c) To 1 pound (or $\frac{1}{2}$ kilo) of flour—2 eggs
2 level teaspoons ginger or spice
1 level teaspoon bicarbonate
of soda or 2 level teaspoons
baking powder
$\frac{1}{2}$ pint (250 ml) milk or water.

12 Fat, sugar and syrup are warmed gently in the pan until they melt.

13 325–350 °F (170–180 °C), Gas Mark 3–4. (Reduce temperature to finish baking.)

14 Gingerbread, parkin, malt loaf.

15 They should be evenly coloured.
Firm when pressed lightly.
Large cakes shrunk a little from sides of the tin.
There should be no sound of hissing.

16 Plain—about 2–3 days.
Rich—several days.
Rich fruit—several weeks.
Fatless sponge—best eaten same day.
Gingerbread—best kept a day before cutting.

17 Add egg at room temperature, gradually.

Scones

1 The rubbing-in method.

2 $\frac{1}{8}$–$\frac{1}{4}$ fat to flour (plain).
$\frac{1}{8}$ sugar to flour ($\frac{1}{8}$ fruit for fruit scones).
$\frac{1}{4}$ pint liquid to $\frac{1}{2}$ pound flour (or 125 ml to 200 g).
Raising agent—4 level teaspoons baking powder to $\frac{1}{2}$ pound
(or 200 g) of flour.
or 1 level teaspoon of bicarbonate of soda.
plus 2 level teaspoons of cream of tartar.

or If using sour milk to mix, use 1 level teaspoon of cream of tartar plus 1 level teaspoon of bicarbonate of soda.

3   Electric 450 °F (230 °C), Gas Mark 8.

4   Small 10 minutes. Large 15 minutes.

5   Cheese, potato, treacle, fruit.

6   About $\frac{3}{4}$ inch (2 cm) thick.

Biscuits

1   According to the method used for making them, as a rule, e.g. creaming, rubbing-in, etc.

2   Not as a rule.

3   To prevent them from rising.

4   No, because they absorb moisture and become soft.

Beverages

1   Their food value is small unless milk and sugar are added.

2   Indian, China, Ceylon.

3   Caffeine stimulates.

4   Tannin hardens protein. This makes protein harder to digest. Many people will not drink tea at or after a meal which contained protein food.

5   As coffee beans, ground coffee, instant coffee and coffee essence.

6   It is not as stimulating as tea and coffee and it contains little tannin.

7   Ovaltine, Benger's food, Nesquick, Milo, Horlick's, etc.

8 They are usually made with milk. They often have added nutrients, e.g. vitamins.

9 If they are made of fresh citrus fruits they will contain some vitamin C.
If sugar is used as a sweetener, it will give some added energy. Whatever the drinks are made of they can be useful to get people to drink plenty of liquid.

Flavouring Food

1 Tastes of several spices.
Used mainly in savoury dishes.
Sold whole or ground.
Don't confuse "Allspice" with "Mixed spice".

2 The bark of a type of laurel tree.
Used in cakes and biscuits as well as in chutneys and sauces.
Sold powdered or in little sticks.

3 The dried unopened flower buds of a tropical tree.
Used in apple pie, chutney, soups and stews.

4 A mixture of several spices.
Tastes very hot.
Used in curries, sauces and soups.

5 Prepared from the underground stem of a tropical plant.
Used in cakes, biscuits and pickles. Also as an accompaniment to melon.
Sold as root ginger, preserved ginger and ground ginger.

6 The kernel of the nutmeg tree, grown in the East and West Indies.
Used grated over custards, junkets and milk puddings.
Sold whole or ground.

7 Extracted from the kernel of bitter almonds.
Used to flavour cakes, puddings and sweets.

8 Sold as oil of peppermint.
Used for sweets and icings.

9 Extracted from vanilla pods.
The pods may be used whole, e.g. to flavour milk for milk puddings.
The essence is usually used for cakes, puddings and icings.

10 Comes from a type of laurel tree.
Used in custards and milk puddings. Also in sauces and stews.

11 Have a mild onion flavour.
Used in salads, soups, omelettes and as a garnish.

12 Belongs to the onion family.
Has a very strong flavour.
The dried bulb is made up of sections called "Cloves".
The cloves are crushed with a knife and finely chopped for use.
Used in savoury dishes and salads.

13 Has a strong flavour.
Used mainly in stuffing for pork and duck.

14 Used in stuffing for veal, fish or chicken.
Also used in soups, stews, sauces and omelettes.

Gelatine

1 A substance made from the bones and hooves of young animals. It is purified and dried.
It is used for setting sweet and savoury jellies.

2 Usually in powdered form, sometimes in sheet form.

3 Gelatine is a protein food but is incomplete because it does not contain all the essential amino acids.
When it is mixed with other food containing incomplete proteins the food value of both is increased.
Gelatine is useful in invalid cookery.
It is useful for making nourishing dishes when used with milk, eggs, meat or fruit.

4 Always measure gelatine carefully. The little packets of powdered gelatine are a help.
Dissolve gelatine in a little cold or warm water—not boiling water.
Don't boil gelatine.
Add it to mixtures slowly.
Pour gelatine mixtures into moulds when cold and beginning to thicken.

5 A savoury jelly.
Can be made from meat or chicken stocks with added gelatine.
Egg whites and shells are used to clear the jelly.
May also be bought in packets.

6 Sweet jellies, fruit, milk, etc.
Moulds—meat or vegetable.
For glazing flans.
Cold soufflés.
Stock for pies.

Convenience Foods

1 Bottled sauce, custard powder, jellies, dried milk, canned soups.

2 Usually easy to carry and easy to store.
Save time.   Sometimes save money.
Give variety to meals.   Better than poor cooking.
No waste.

3 Often expensive.
Temptation to use them more often than necessary.
They sometimes get used to the exclusion of fresh foods.
Some people easily tire of them because they always taste the same.
They are mostly soft foods.

4 Buy with care—refuse broken packets, badly dented tins, etc.
If the food does not smell or look fresh don't use it.
Follow directions for use exactly.

Store according to instructions.
Never keep the food longer than instructed, opened or
unopened.

Preservation

1 To destroy the destructive organisms in food or to prevent
them growing.
To prevent others reaching the food.

2 The decay of food is caused by the following:
Enzymes.   Moulds.
Yeasts.   Bacteria.

3 They are chemical substances present in all living matter.

4 No, but they spoil food, e.g. cause fruit and vegetables
to become over-ripe and decay.

5 (a) High temperature destroys them.
    (b) Cold checks their growth.

6 They are single-cell plants which multiply by budding.

7 In the air and on the skins of fruit.

8 Warmth, moisture, sugary substances.

9 (a) High temperature kills them.
    (b) Low temperature checks their growth.

10 They are tiny plants.

11 They are present in the air and they settle on food.

12 Warm, moist conditions.

13 Cold, dry storage, high temperature, acetic acid, sulphur
dioxide.

14 Tiny plants, smallest of all living things.

15 Food, warmth, moisture.

16 (a) Destroyed by very high temperature.
(b) Low temperature, acids and strong solutions of sugar and salt.

17 Yes, by producing poisonous toxins.

18 Heat.
Cold.
Drying.
Adding salt, sugar, or other chemical preservatives.

19 Most fruits are suitable.
It is not safe to bottle vegetables unless a pressure cooker is used, because a high enough temperature cannot be reached without one.

20 Use best fruit.
Prepare carefully.
Use perfect jars, and new rubber bands (if used).
Pack carefully.
Sterilise in oven, water bath or pressure cooker.
Bottles must be about 2 inches (5 cm) apart.
The seal must be tested the next day. If the jars have not been sealed properly they must be re-processed or the fruit used as stewed fruit.

21 This is usually done commercially but may also be done at home:
Foods may be meat, fish, vegetables, puddings, etc.
Tins are made of sheet steel and lined with tin.
Only best quality food must be used.
There is not much loss of vitamins.

22 That some organisms are not destroyed. They can grow again when the food is thawed.

23 Very low temperature.
Small ice crystals.
Food does not break up or lose its flavour.
Food frozen by this method—meat, fish, poultry, soft fruit, vegetables, cream cakes, etc.

24 (a) Means Accelerated Freeze Drying.
It is a method of preserving food by combining the two methods of quick freezing and drying food.
(b) Flavour is kept.
The normal texture and colour are kept.
Nutrients not lost.
No special storage space needed.
Easy to carry home.
Easy to prepare and cook.

25 Moisture is removed from the food:
May be done commercially, e.g. milk, soup, potatoes, eggs, meat, vegetables, fruit, etc.
At home—herbs and apple rings.
Dried foods need to be stored in airtight containers—they spoil if allowed to become damp.

26 Sugar, salt, vinegar, sulphur dioxide.

27 Fruit and sugar.

28 Found in the cell walls of young fruit and vegetables.
Helps to set jam.

29 Citrus fruits, blackcurrants, gooseberries, plums, cooking apples.

30 Blackberries, pears, strawberries.

31 By adding fruits or juices rich in pectin, e.g. lemon juice, cooking apples.
By using commercial pectin, e.g. Certo.

32 Put a teaspoon of cooked fruit juice in a tumbler.
Leave to cool.
Add 3 teaspoons of methylated spirit.
Shake the tumbler.
Leave about a minute.
Check result.
Rich in pectin—one lump of jelly is formed.
Moderate amount—2 or 3 pieces formed.
Poor amount—lots of little pieces formed.

33 Cook slowly before adding the sugar.
Cook quickly after adding the sugar.

34 Cold plate, flake, thermometer, weighing.

35 In a cool, dry, dark place.

Definitions

1 A dish is covered with sauce.
Breadcrumbs or cheese (or both) are sprinkled over the top.
The dish is browned under the grill or in the oven.

2 To bake pastry cases without any filling in them. (Beans are put in to stop them rising.)

3 To spoon hot fat or other liquid over food whilst cooking.
It is done to keep the food moist.

4 Food is covered with cold water and brought to the boil.
Then it is strained and rinsed in cold water.

5 To mix smoothly. It usually refers to a starchy powder being mixed with a liquid.

6 A small bunch of the following herbs tied together and used to flavour soups and stews: parsley, thyme, marjoram and bay leaf.

7 Bread cut into fancy shapes or dice and then fried.

8 Stuffing, e.g. sage and onion.

9 Decorating savoury dishes.
It is done to add colour and flavour, and to make the food appetising. May also add extra food value. Tomato and parsley are examples of garnishes.

10 Food is glazed to give it a glossy appearance.
Some glazes are: egg, sugar and water, thickened fruit juices.
Savoury as well as sweet foods may be glazed.
Foods glazed include pies, buns, scones and flans.

11 A mixture of fruit or vegetables cut into dice.

12 Food is partly cooked by boiling and then the cooking may be finished by another method, e.g. potatoes are often partboiled and then roasted.

13 Fat and flour are cooked together (usually in equal quantities). The mixture is used to thicken sauces, soups and stews.

14 Food cooked by being tossed in a little hot fat, e.g. potatoes.

15 The thin outside skin of citrus fruits.
It contains the oil which gives the flavour.

Failures in Cooking

CAKES
1 Oven door opened too soon.
Oven door slammed.
Cake moved before it had set.
Taken out of the oven too soon.
Oven too cool.
Too much liquid used in mixing.
Too much raising agent.
The fruit was wet.
The fat, sugar and eggs were over-creamed. This can happen if a mixer is used.

2 Wet fruit used.
Mixture too slack.
Oven too cool.

3 The oven was too hot.
Cooked on too high a shelf.

PASTRY
4 Over kneading—or over rolling.
Pastry turned over.
Too much flour used when the pastry was rolled out.
Too much water was used.
Pastry cooked too slowly.

5 Too much water was used.
Not kept cool enough.
Too much flour used when the pastry was rolled out.
Over rolling.
The oven was not hot enough.

6 Uneven folding and rolling.
Fat not distributed evenly.
Edges not cut off before the pastry was used.
The pastry was not left to relax long enough between rollings or before baking.

7 Pastry was stretched too much when it was rolled or shaped.
Not allowed to relax long enough between rollings or before baking.

8 Not enough baking powder or liquid.
Baked instead of steamed.
Baked too quickly.

9 Not enough baking powder.
Pastry got wet during cooking.

BREAD
10 Liquid too hot—so the yeast was killed.

11 The dough was put in too hot a place for the first rising.

12 The oven was not hot enough to start with.
The dough was proved too long.

13 Stale yeast or too much yeast.
Rising and proving too slow.

SAUCES
14 Roux—Fat too hot when flour added.
Liquid added too quickly.
Liquid and roux not mixed properly.
Blended—Liquid added too quickly.
Powder and liquid not blended properly.

15 Roux not cooked long enough.
Sauce not cooked long enough.

16 The sauce was not cooked long enough after the liquid was added.

17 Wrong proportion of ingredients.
Over or under cooking.

JAM
18 Not enough pectin or acid in the fruit. Lemon juice should have been added.

19 Jam put in the pots whilst it was too hot.

20 Covered whilst still warm.
Too little sugar.
Stored in a damp place.

21 Not enough acid in fruit.
Too much sugar used.
Jam boiled too long or not long enough.

BOTTLING
22 Too much sugar in the syrup.
Temperature raised too quickly.
Too loosely packed.

23 Bottles not heated enough.
Heating at too low a temperature.
Temperature raised too quickly.

FRYING
24 Fat not hot enough or not drained.

25 Fat not strained after it was used last.

26 Coating not put on evenly or fat not hot enough.

27 Fat too hot so that the outside looks done before the inside is cooked.

GENERAL

28 Too hot milk added to the egg.
Custard overheated.

29 The milk was too hot when the rennet was added.
The junket was not put in a warm place to set.
Junket was moved before it was set.

PEOPLE

Babies

1   Food, sleep, fresh air, being kept clean.

2   To be loved and wanted.
    To be kept safe and comfortable.

3   Waiting for food.
    Being treated roughly.
    Feeling as if they are falling.
    Sudden loud bangs.

4   Yes because babies don't understand what's going on.
    They get fretful if they lose their sleep or have to wait
    for their food.

5   How to get the mother quickly.
    How to get a doctor quickly.
    All the safety rules for babies.
    The everyday rules for looking after babies, how to feed
    them, change them, etc.
    That it is not safe to go baby sitting if you are not well,
    e.g. if you have a bad cold, sore throat, upset stomach, etc.

6   Always tell the mother where you are going.
    Never leave the baby by itself.
    Don't let other girls handle it.
    If it has the smallest accident you must tell the mother.

7   (a) Loving   Hating
         Happy   Unhappy
         Angry   Pleased
         Jealous   Afraid/Lonely.
    (b) Yes.

8   Really grown-up people try to control their feelings and
    usually do so. Small children just behave as they feel.

9   Yes. It is very important that older people should let small
    children know they still love them after they have been
    angry with them and everything has "blown over".

10 Yes, he should have a safe night-light as long as he is afraid of the dark.

11 He should have his fair share of attention.
He should be allowed to "share" in the baby.
He should always have a special little fuss made of him at bedtime.
He should have one or two little gifts "to celebrate" the baby's coming.

12 By asking questions.
By being taught.
By playing.
By watching other children and grown-ups.

13 Show them how to do things for themselves.
Teach them how to take care of their things.
Teach them how to play by themselves.
Allow them to explore places and things as long as there is no real danger.

Children–Safety

1 Windows—Fix vertical bars.
Balconies—Board them in to a suitable height.
Tables—Don't leave babies alone on tables even for a minute.
Stairs—Fix gates at top and bottom. Fix a low handrail on one side.
Floors—Must be non-slip with no loose rugs.

2 Use safety straps.
Don't overload prams with shopping. Safer to have a tray under the pram.
Make sure the brakes are in good working order.
Cot sides must have childproof fastenings.

3 Put non-slip mats in the bath and on the floor.
Fix a safety rail or child's bath seat in the bath.
Make the lavatory chain longer.

4 Shoes and slippers should be well fitting and properly fastened.
Trousers should have shoulder straps to prevent them slipping down and causing the child to trip.

5 Opened tins, broken glass and china.
Sharp and pointed tools and sewing equipment.
Jewellery with sharp edges or pins.
Knives, razor blades, compasses, pens, etc.

6 (a) Use safety power points or fit dummy plugs.
(b) Keep them as short as possible and fix them to skirting boards where possible.
(c) Don't let small children turn electric blankets on or off.
(d) Place the set where a small child can't get behind it.
(e) The general rule is, never leave small children and electric appliances together.

7

Alcohol	Fuel oils	Medical supplies
Anti-freeze	Garden sprays	Perfumes
Bad food	Coal gas	Poisonous plants
Beauty aids	Household cleaners	Rat poison
Decorating things		

8 Keep them locked up when not in use.
Don't leave a child with them when they are being used.
Get rid of poisonous plants from the garden.
Teach children not to eat anything from the garden without "showing Mummie first".
It's safer not to give small children little sips of alcohol.

9 Yes, they can be poisoned by such things as the following:
Vitamin pills, slimming tablets, seasickness pills, birth control pills and laxatives.

10 Have safety taps fitted on cookers and fires.

11 Yes, these things must be kept away from little children:
dry-cleaning fluid, shoe polish, furniture polish, metal polish, etc.

12 When they are hungry or bored and when they are left alone.

13 Yes, this is possible. It is always safer to ask the clinic or doctor which ointments or dusting powder to use on a baby.

14 When hot liquid is spilt on them or they pull hot liquid on to themselves.
By falling into hot water, e.g. coppers.
By being put into baths which are too hot.
If they eat or drink anything which is too hot.

15 Never put hot liquids near little children and never put little children anywhere where there are hot liquids.

16 Don't use tablecloths, or—
Thread elastic through the hem so that the cloth just fits the table top.
Don't put hot liquids near the edge of the table.

17 Always put the cold water in the bath first.
When the bath is ready, test the water with your elbow.
Try not to get the bath water ready if a toddler is about.
Never add hot water to a bath whilst a child is in the bath.
Small children must never be left alone in the bath.

18 No, because the baby might move and make you spill the hot liquid over him.

19 Never fill bottles with very hot water.
Check them carefully.
Put a thick cover on and put them beneath the under-blanket.

20 Use safety pillows in their cots and prams.
Tuck the bedclothes in tightly.
Always put the baby to sleep alone in his own cot or pram.
Check collapsible cots often.
Fix safety nets on prams and cots to keep animals and insects out.
Never leave a small child alone with its bottle or other food.

21 Keep all plastic bags right away from small children even if the bags have holes in them.
Never put children's toys in plastic bags.

Take them off mattresses, toys, etc., as soon as you get the goods home.

Don't use pieces of plastic sheeting in cots and prams.

Safer not to use plastic bibs, but if they are used they must be taken off the baby as soon as the meal is finished.

22 Don't air clothes too near the fire.
Never burn fabric on a fire if the baby is in the room.
Be very careful to see that unlit gas taps are not left on.
Keep a check on boilers, oil and gas fires to make sure that they are working properly.
Don't leave babies or little children in a room if the fire is smoking.

23 Always have a safe guard up if there are children in the house.
Put portable fires in the safest place.
Don't allow small children to turn fires on.
Don't let small children come into the room when the fire is being lit or made up.
Never leave a small child in the room with an oil heater.

24 Battery operated ones are best.
Any others must be put in a safe place out of the child's reach and out of draughts.

25 Keep matches and lighters away from small children at all times.

26 Safety taps should be fitted to cookers.
Gas lighters and "guns" which hang on the sides of some cookers should be removed if there are toddlers in the house.
It is safer to use battery lighters instead of matches.

27 Little children must not be allowed to touch fireworks or bonfires.
Older children must be told not to light fireworks, even "sparklers", near small children.

28 As many of the child's clothes as possible should be made of flame resisting material.
This is particularly important for party dresses and nightwear.

29 Small babies must not be left in the hot sun to burn.
Put the pram in a shady place and check often.
Sun-bathing—
Five minutes a day is long enough to start with. When the
baby is tanned he should still only have short sunbathes
and always wear a hat.

30 Make sure the person knows how to take care of babies
properly.
Don't leave babies with young children.
Don't leave the baby with anybody who doesn't like it.
Let the person know where they can find you if necessary.

31 Many people grow up into responsible adults without
being hit.
Babies must never be hit.
Never hit a child if you are in a temper.
Children must never be punched, kicked or hit with hard
objects.
Children must not be hit anywhere where real damage may
be caused, e.g. on the head.

32 Yes, because if they are not they can be badly hurt.

33 Small babies never do anything out of spite or to be
annoying.

34 No, small babies never do these things because they are
naughty. They just don't understand.

35 Children's clinics. Health visitors, midwives, doctors. Also
Mothercare lessons at school, Parentcraft courses at evening
school and books on Child Care.

36 The National Society for the Prevention of Cruelty to
Children.

37 Smallpox, diphtheria, whooping cough, measles, tuber-
culosis, poliomyelitis.

38 By keeping all the rules of general hygiene in the home.
Giving the baby good, clean food of the right kind, in the
right amounts.

Keeping the baby and everything that touches him clean.
Keeping the baby happy.
Getting all the help she can to keep him well and happy.

39 Do not let children touch animal's food or the animal's box.
Always wash a small child's hands after he has been playing
with an animal, especially before the child has a meal.

40 Ring the doctor at once and tell him the child's symptoms.

41 The child must have a safe place to play in.
His toys must be safe.
He should be taught how to play safely.
If he is playing with water, or with or near something which
may be dangerous, he must be watched all the time.

42 Make sure the fences and gate are in good condition so that
the child cannot get out of the garden.
Remove any poisonous plants.
Keep all water firmly covered unless you are watching the
child play with it.
Make sure there are no broken flower pots, etc., around, and
no dangerous tools.
If possible fence a part of the garden off for very little
children so that they can be within sight of the house all the
time.

43 Buy the right toys for the child's age group.
Look for safety and hygiene labels.

44 Check them often to see that they are not broken, and
showing sharp or pointed parts.
Check for roughness, nails sticking out, etc.
Keep an eye on toys other children bring in.

45 (a) Make sure they are not inflammable.
Check for washing labels.
Check that the eyes or other parts won't come off.
May be safer to take the eyes out and embroider eyes
on.
Make sure the arms and legs and head are not fixed
on with wire.
(b) Check them often for splinters, any roughness, nails,
loose screws and joints which may have come undone.

46 The paint—they must not be painted with lead paint.

47 Never let them out alone.
Strap toddlers into pushchairs.
Don't leave prams out of your sight.
Teach them their name and address as soon as possible.
Use a leading-rein for toddlers.
Sew their name, address and telephone number on to their underclothes.
Let them wear an identity bracelet that they can't undo.

48 Always cross at the proper crossing places.
Teach the child kerb drill as soon as possible.
Always do kerb drill yourself out loud for the child to hear.

49 Keep hold of them all the time.
Teach them the proper way to get on and off buses, escalators, etc.
When waiting for buses or trains, don't let the child stand on the kerb side or on the platform edge.

50 The "Tufty Club". Get information from the Royal Society for the Prevention of Accidents.

51 Obedience.
Safe and tidy habits.
Self-reliance.
How to use dangerous things properly.
How to recognise danger.
How to read and recognise safety signs and symbols.
Safety skills such as swimming, floating, falling correctly, etc.
Where and how to get help.

Menfolk

1 How to manage the family income.
Choosing furniture and equipment for the home.
How to choose and how to buy the right food.
A little cookery.
Some laundry and housework—how to do the everyday jobs.
How to look after the rest of the family if the mother is ill.

2 Materials which will wear well and always look smart.
Materials which are easy to wash and need little or no ironing.
Clothes which small boys will not grow out of too soon.
Clothes which are suitable for the occasion.
Clothes which are fashionable, especially for boys who are growing up.

3 By giving them a well-balanced diet of well-cooked, interesting foods.
They can try to see that the husband gets enough rest of the kind he needs, e.g. heavy physical work needs extra rest and sleep.
Men who do a worrying job need plenty of sleep and non-worrying things to think about.

4 Citizens' Advice Bureau.
Marriage Guidance Council branches.

Old People

1 Make sure they get the care of a doctor when they need it.
See that they get all they need of the following and that they are kept in good condition:
Teeth, glasses, hearing aids, special equipment if they are disabled.
They should also have their feet looked after by a chiropodist if necessary.
You should take a very old person for a little walk at least once a day.

2 Go shopping for them.
Help to get the food ready.
Eat with them at least sometimes.
See that they get a well-balanced diet.

3 Get them clothes which are:
Warm in winter but not too heavy.
Cool in summer but not too skimpy.
Easy to get on and off.
Easy to care for.
Nice looking.

4 (a) Comb and brush it gently.

Shampoo and set it carefully.

Give or get the hairdresser to give them a light perm now and again.

(b) Do their nails for them regularly.

Give them some hand cream or put it on for them.

(c) Keep their toenails short.

Get them a footbath ready every now and again.

5 Visit them and do any jobs they want you to do.

Do shopping.

Change library books.

Take their dog for walks or brush their cat or clean out their bird's cage.

6 Make them feel they are always one of the family.

Look after them without fussing.

Let them know what is going on in the home.

Make sure they have at least some of their own things around.

See that everybody in the home respects them.

7 Put their bed and chair out of draughts.

Give them warm but light-weight bedclothes.

Provide them with electric blankets and hot water bottles (covered).

See that their room is properly heated.

8 They should have the safest kind of fire and it must be well guarded.

If the fire is an open fire it should be made up for a very old person. Oil fires should be filled and cleaned for them too.

Their beds and armchairs should not be too close to the fire.

They should have large, deep ashtrays which stand firm.

As many as possible of the materials for their clothes, bedclothes and furnishings should be made of non-flare material.

9 If possible they should not have to do jobs with boiling or very hot water.

Baths should be run for them and hot water bottles should be filled for them.

Any pans and kettles they use should be small and light, whenever possible.
Pans and kettles of boiling liquid should not be left where an old person might knock them accidentally.

10 Somebody should see that all their gas fittings and appliances are checked by the Gas Board for safety.
Their gas taps should be checked every night.
To save them getting up in the night to make tea, etc., they should be given a flask each night.
There should be at least a little ventilation in any room where a gas appliance is being used.
If the old person lives alone they need frequent visitors to see that they are all right and to keep an eye on their gas equipment.

11 There should be no slippery floors and nothing left about on floors to trip up old people.
The lighting should be good everywhere.
There should be extra handrails on the wall side of stairs, by back door steps, in bathrooms and toilets and anywhere else an old person is likely to lose their balance.
Beds and chairs should be the right height.
Their things should not be put on high shelves.
Very old people should be encouraged to use a stick.

12 Generally speaking, other people have got to do it for them.
They should always have somebody with them outdoors, especially in busy streets.
Road safety rules should be explained to them and any new rules as they come out.

13 Their medicine should be given to them.
If they live alone their medicine should have the directions on the bottle, etc., in large letters.

14 Good visitors are the most useful help to the old person living alone.
Other helps are a telephone, SOS cards that can be put in the window if the old person needs help, and flashing signals that the old person can switch on if he needs help.
It is the duty of neighbours to keep an eye on old people in a nice way to see if they are all right, e.g. have the papers been taken in, or the milk bottles left out, etc.

15 Very old people should not go further than they can be seen
if they are taking out little babies in prams.
It is not safe to leave lively toddlers in the charge of a very
old person.

Personal Hygiene

1 To clean away dirt and grease.
To wash away stale perspiration.
To remove dead skin.
To get rid of germs.

2 Clean them at least once a day, with an up-and-down
movement.
Don't crack nuts with them.
Visit the dentist regularly.
Drink plenty of milk.
Eat foods rich in calcium.
Eat fruit rich in vitamin C.
Take cod liver oil.
Eat plenty of crispy foods.

3 Wash it regularly.
Brush it daily and comb it often.
Be careful with hair sprays and colourings and perms.
Keep your brush and comb clean.
Have it properly cut.
Keep all the hygiene rules for general fitness.

4 Comb the hairs out of the brush.
Wash the brush and comb in warm soapy water.
Rinse well.
Dry nylon combs and brushes on a towel.
Hang natural bristle brushes up to dry.

5 Never to push things into the nose.
Not to play with it.
To use a handkerchief when necessary and not to blow the
nose too hard.

6 Never push anything into them.
Keep them clean inside and outside.

See the doctor if you have pains in your ears or get a discharge.
Never hit people's ears.

7   Wear glasses if you need to.
Never read in a bad light.
Don't rub your eyes if you get something in them.
Never look straight at the sun—wear sunglasses if the sun is very strong.
Keep all the rules of general hygiene.

8   Wash them often.
Keep any cuts wrapped up.
Cut the nails short and keep them clean.
Wear gloves for dirty work.
Wear gloves in cold weather.
Use a little hand cream at night.

9   Wash them daily and dry them well.
Wear the correct size in socks, stockings and shoes.
Walk round with bare feet when it's safe to do so.
Rest your feet by putting them up, especially if you stand all day.
Soak them if they get hot and swollen.
Use medicated foot powder or talcum powder if you walk a lot.

10 Buy comfortable well-fitting shoes, slippers and boots the correct size.
Keep them in good repair.
Dry them away from strong heat.
Clean them often.
Store them carefully.
If possible have more than one pair of walking shoes.

11 It improves the circulation and appetite.
Helps muscles to develop.
Enables you to breathe more deeply and get more oxygen.
It helps the body to get rid of waste.

12 Because correct posture helps you to breathe better and to digest your food better.

It also helps to keep the spine straight and prevent muscular strain.
It makes you look better.

13 Sleep helps the body to recover from the day's wear and tear.
If the body gets enough sleep it can work better.
Enough sleep also helps the mind to think clearly and quickly.
Every part of the body is helped by sleep and every part of the body suffers if a person does not get enough sleep.

14 Remove stains at once.
Mend tears straight away.
Keep your clothes well brushed and always hung carefully on hangers or folded away.
Clothes should always be worn carefully and changed when the person comes indoors, except for leisure clothes.
All clothes must be kept clean and well pressed.

15 The following points should be considered when buying clothes:
They should be the right size and well fitting and comfortable.
They should be well made, of easy-care material.
Clothes should always suit the person who wears them.
Clothes should be suitable for the occasion.
They should also be warm in winter, cool in summer and waterproof in wet weather.

16 Fresh air is necessary to keep the body healthy.
It helps perspiration to evaporate and keeps the skin fresh.
It also helps to keep the skin at the right temperature.
If people get enough fresh air they have alert minds, they sleep well, eat well, and feel healthy.
Sunshine makes people feel well and bright as a rule.
It also provides the body with vitamin D.

17 Buy easy-care materials.
Wash and change them daily.
Keep them tidily in a drawer and mend them when necessary.

18 Buy clothes which don't show every mark.
See that they are made of easy-care materials.
Keep them in good repair.

19 Turn them out regularly.
Keep them clean inside and out.
Use small size things that don't take up much room.
Keep small things in little cosmetic bags.
Don't use ordinary handbags to put the shopping in.

20 Go to bed if you have a cold.
Use a handkerchief if you cough or sneeze.
Don't breathe over other people.
Don't go to places where there are a lot of people.

21 By taking *regular* care of your body and clothes.

22 Good hygiene is the base of all beauty care.

23 Always use the best for your skin.
Remove all make-up every night.
Keep everything you use for making-up very clean.
Only use make-up which improves you.
Always wear the correct make-up for the occasion.

24 Most people, unless they can wash often each day, do need to use a deodorant as well as washing and bathing.

25 Go to see the doctor at once, because he can easily cure it.

26 Bad breath can be prevented by:
Keeping the teeth clean and healthy.
Eating the right food and digesting it properly.
Not smoking.

27 Because they may be suffering from pre-menstrual tension.
They should:
See the doctor.
Go to bed early for a few nights.

28 Go to see the doctor.

29 By keeping yourself busy.
By helping other people.
By keeping all the hygiene rules, especially getting enough sleep.

30 The Duke of Edinburgh's Award Scheme, Indoor and outdoor sport, First Aid, Evening school subjects, Music, Art, reading, collecting (e.g. stamps).

Accidents

1 Dettol or T.C.P.
Burn dressing.
Anti-histamine ointment.
Bandages—2 triangular; 1 each of—1 inch (2·5 cm), 2 inch (5 cm), 3 inch (7·5 cm), + 1 crêpe 3 inch (7·5 cm).
Roll of gauze.
Cotton wool.
Lint.
Wound dressings—various sizes.
Adhesive plaster.
Scissors with rounded ends.
Pair of tweezers.
Safety pins—various sizes.
Small bowl and eye bath.
Graduated medicine glass.
The doctor's telephone number on the lid.

2 Everything to be used for First Aid purposes only.
Keep the box and everything in it very clean.
Keep the things tidy. Rewrap packets, etc., after use.
Replace articles before the last is used up so as not to run out of anything.
Make sure you know your kit. Read instructions on packets, etc., before you need to use them, as well as when the time comes to treat an injury.

3 As many members of the family as possible should learn First Aid.
There should be a well-fitted First Aid box in the home.
Everybody should know how to get help when necessary.

4 The doctor's telephone number.
The nearest telephone if you haven't one.
A reliable taxi telephone number.

The quickest way to the doctor's surgery and the Hospital Casualty department.
Which neighbour will help in an emergency.

5   If the injured person is likely to get hurt again they should be moved from where they are—otherwise do not move them.
The doctor should be sent for at once.
Artificial respiration must be given if breathing has stopped.
Bad bleeding must be stopped quickly.
Don't give alcohol, or food or drink (except in the case of burns if the patient is quite conscious). See p. 124 No. 10.
Keep people from crowding around.
Don't take the person's clothes off unless really necessary.
Make the person feel confident.

6   Wash under the tap.
Pat dry with clean cotton or linen material.
Put a piece of adhesive plaster on it.
If it does not heal properly let the doctor see it.

7   Send for the doctor.
Lay the person down. Cover with a blanket, except the part which is bleeding.
Raise the cut part on a cushion.
Press a pad of clean material on to the wound to stop the bleeding. If there is glass in the wound take it out, if this is easy. If you can't take the glass or whatever it is out, press *round* the wound.

8   Sit the person by an open window.
Loosen his clothes round the neck and chest.
Tell him to breathe through his mouth.
Tell him to hold his nose (do this for a small child).
Call the doctor if the nose is still bleeding badly after about 15 minutes.
Always call the doctor in the case of an elderly person.

9   Hold the burnt part under the running cold tap for about ten minutes.
Put a special burn dressing on, or suitable burn ointment.
If it doesn't heal properly let the doctor see it.

10 Pull the person away from the heat, e.g. out of the boiling liquid, or remove the cause of burning, e.g. a hot coal.
Call the doctor or take the person to the casualty department of the hospital, whichever is quickest.
Check the patient for fainting, loss of breathing, etc., and treat if necessary.
If the patient is conscious give little sips of water until the doctor comes or until they get to hospital (glass of water $+$ $\frac{1}{2}$ teaspoon of salt and a pinch of bicarbonate of soda).

11 If the person has fallen down—lay them flat and turn their head to one side.
Otherwise the person may be sat in a chair and his head bent down between his knees.
Give the patient plenty of fresh air to breathe.
Put a blanket round him if it's very cold.
Give a warm drink when they feel a little better (no sugar if they don't like it).
Don't give the person aspirin and don't leave them alone.
If the patient takes a very long time to come round, or keeps fainting, send for the doctor.

12 *Don't* move it round and round to see if it is broken.
Either take the person to the casualty department of the hospital or call the doctor.
Whilst you are waiting for the doctor—keep the person still.
Cover them if they feel cold. Don't give them food or drink.

13 Call the doctor or take the person to a hospital casualty department.
If you can't get help soon, give them water to drink if they are conscious. Keep them lying on one side to prevent them being choked by vomit.
If the person seems to get better quite soon he should still be seen by a doctor, especially children.
If there is some of the poisonous substance left, take it to the doctor.
If the person is sick take that to the doctor too (in a plastic bag).

14 Turn off the electricity and pull out the plug, if possible.
Pull the person away. Don't touch the person's body with your hands or any part of your body.

Use something made of rubber or wood to touch them (not an umbrella if it has metal on it). Or pull a loose part of their clothing.

It may be possible to pull the appliance away by its flex but don't touch the appliance.

Send for the doctor if somebody hasn't already done so.

If the person is not breathing, give artificial respiration.

15 Put a anti-histamine ointment or lotion on.

16 Carry them out of the water so that the water can run out of their mouth.

Begin artificial respiration at once.

You may have to clear the person's mouth of weeds, etc. first. You may be able to save vital seconds by giving artificial respiration whilst the person is still in the water.

Send for the doctor or ambulance if somebody hasn't already done so.

17 Call the doctor.

Lay the child down with his head to one side.

Cover him with a blanket. Stay with him.

18 Send for the doctor.

Lay the person in a cool place—head up.

Cool them quickly—clothes off, fan body, wipe body with cold water.

If you have to wait for the doctor give the patient a glass of water with a $\frac{1}{4}$ teaspoon of salt in it.

19 Don't touch the eye if it is bleeding. Take the person to the casualty department of the hospital or call the doctor at once.

Dust—

Damp the corner of a clean handkerchief and gently try to get the dust out. if it won't come out the person must see the doctor.

Cleaning liquids or anything else liquid you think will be dangerous—

Hold the head to one side, bad side lowest.

Keep running cold water into the eye.

The patient must go to the hospital casualty department or be seen by a doctor at once.

20 If the person is not choking, call the doctor or take the person to the casualty department.
If they are choking—
Get someone to call the doctor.
Bend the person's shoulders forward and thump them between the shoulder-blades. Turn children upside down and slap them between the shoulder-blades.

21 Send for the doctor.
Wrap the baby in blankets and carry it into a warm room.
Give it a warm drink if it is conscious.
Don't put it too near the fire and don't use hot water bottles.
If the baby is unconscious and not breathing give mouth-to-mouth respiration.

Home Nursing

1 Write the message down.

2 Be spotlessly clean.
Keep yourself well.
Be cheerful.
Always be kind and gentle.
Do everything quietly.
Be very observant.
Never talk about the patient's health where he can hear.

3 To do exactly what the doctor says.

4 Visit at the right time (ask first).
Don't tire the patient.
Ask what kind of things the patient can have and don't bring anything else.
Don't sit on the bed.
Don't eat the patient's food or drink anything in the sickroom.
Stay the correct length of time.
Make sure the patient is better for the person's visit.
Don't talk about illness all the time.

5 You should choose a quiet room.
It should be near the bathroom and the lavatory.

The room should be pleasant, not too hot and not too cold.
If the patient has a contagious illness he should be in a
room as far away from the rest of the family rooms
as possible.

6   It means he wants some of the patient's urine in a bottle so
that he can take it away to be tested.
The urine should be put in a clean bottle and corked.
A label should be stuck on with the patient's name on it,
the patient's address and the date.

7   Take out any unnecessary things if possible.
Put the bed in a place which is not in a draught and not
too near any heating.
The head of the bed should not face the window or an
unshaded light all the time.
The nurse should be able to get round the bed easily.
There should be a table and a chair near to the patient's
bed.

8   Do everything quietly.
Take out any food, drink or flowers before you start.
Try not to make the dust fly about.
When you have finished put the patient's things back near
him.
Bring back the flowers in clean water.

9   Bottles should only be half filled.
The top must be very carefully fixed and tested.
A cover should be put on the bottle.
Put it under the under sheet or blanket.
Refill it before it gets too cold.

10 Anything he has asked for.
Washing things, clean towel, etc.
Any notes you have written down about the patient.

Medicine

1   Give the right medicine in the right amount at the right
time.
Always keep the medicine in a safe place.

2   Read the label twice.
    Shake the bottle if it says so.
    Use a graduated medicine glass or spoon.
    Measure out the exact amount (or count the pills).
    Add water to the medicine if told to. (Pour out some water
    for the patient to take the pills with.)
    Watch the patient take the medicine.
    Wash the glass.
    Lock the medicine in the medicine cupboard at once.
    Always keep the label on top when pouring medicines. This
    keeps the label clean.

3   Because they are likely to eat them as sweets if they get
    the chance.

4   It can be very dangerous.
    If somebody does take the wrong medicine and becomes ill
    call the doctor.
    Even if they don't seem ill it's usually best to let a doctor know,
    especially in the case of a child.

5   It may be taken back to the chemist.
    It can be put down the lavatory. (Make sure pills really go
    down.)

6   It usually means the substance is poison.
    It always means the substance must not be put in the mouth
    and swallowed.

7   Must have a lock and key. (Or be otherwise impossible for
    children to open.)
    Must be strong.
    Should have two compartments (one side for poisonous
    substances).
    Better if it has no mirror.

8   Don't get medicines out in the dark.
    Never let small children get medicines out.
    Patients should not get their own medicines out.
    Never put animal's medicines in it.
    Don't use it for everyday first-aid things.
    Never use it for toilet things.
    Keep it locked at all times and keep the key in a safe place.

9 Keep them in the medicine cupboard.
Only give or take them according to directions.
If a person seems very ill only give aspirins if the doctor says so.
Don't give them to anyone who has been unconscious unless the doctor says so.
Don't give them to anybody who says they can't take them.

10 Keep them locked up in a safe medicine cupboard.
Take only one dose into the bedroom.
Never give them to children except by doctor's orders.
Make sure you know whether the person has to take them after getting into bed.

11 Is it all right to take it if you are doing things like driving?
Should you avoid any particular food? (Usually you get a card to tell you if this is so.)
Should you be careful not to drink any alcohol?

Family Safety—Outdoors

1 Yes, it is helpful to all road users.

2 Yes, because children copy.

3 Wear something white.
Face oncoming traffic.

4 Check that the road is clear before pushing the pram into the road.
Always use crossings.
Don't wheel a pram in front of or behind stationary cars, etc., unless you have got to, then be extra careful.

5 The cycle must be safe.
The rider must know and practise the Highway Code.
The rider must always ride in a way which is safe for himself and others.
If anything is being carried on the bicycle it must be firmly fixed and not stick out. It must not prevent the person cycling properly either.
Cyclists should wear clothes which will not catch in the wheels of the cycle and will not prevent the cyclist riding properly.

E

6 Don't try to stop the bus by standing in front of it.
Don't get on or off of moving buses.
Give the proper signal for stopping a bus at request stops.
Also for stopping the bus if you are in it and have to do so.
Don't stand too near the edge of the kerb when waiting for the bus.

7 Obey the rules of the railway company.
Don't stand on the edge of the platform.
Don't open doors before the train stops.
Don't play about at the top or bottom of escalators.

8 The driver must be able to control the car and to control himself.

9 Being drunk, drugged, tired, hungry.
Unable to see or hear properly.
If they are in a temper, showing off, upset, depressed or daydreaming. Being in too much of a hurry.

10 At public holiday times.
When public houses are closing.
When children are coming out of school.
In bad weather.
At dusk and early in the morning.
Near schools and hospitals.

11 They should always wear a safety belt or be in a safety seat.
The back of the car is usually thought the safest place for children, with the doors locked.

12 Make sure they are wearing safety belts.
Make them feel safe by not driving too fast, etc., then they won't get so nervous as to cause an accident.

13 Fire extinguisher.
First aid kit.
Lamp.
Emergency rations, if driving in lonely areas.

14 Disobedience of the school rules.
Long hair, sharp jewellery, high heels.
Fooling about.

15 Obey all the safety rules of the job.
Use common sense.
Do the job correctly and tidily.
No fooling about.
Report faulty equipment at once.
Get minor accidents treated and dressed. Sore fingers, etc.,
can cause major accidents.
Always try to be fit for the job.

16 Obedience of children.
Keep all the general safety rules for indoors and outdoors.
Keep all the safety rules of the area.
If you are going to do something new make sure you know
all about it and have the correct equipment to do it safely.
Make sure cars and other equipment are checked for safety
before the start of the holiday. Pack repair and first aid kits.
Keep as fit as you can.
Make sure everybody knows how and where to get help.

17 Yes, especially children.
Identity bracelets are best.
Information should include name, address (holiday and
home), telephone numbers.

18 You should say where you are going, what you are going
to do, e.g. climb, and what time you expect to be back.

19 They should not swim alone.
Children must be told not to swim straight out to sea.
Children must be able to float for a long time. They should
also know what to do if they fall in the water with their
clothes on.
All swimmers should know of any particular hazards in the
area, e.g. currents.
It is safer not to swim if you are very tired, not well, or if
you have just had a large meal.
Adults must watch children all the time, especially if they
are using floats of any kind.

20 Everybody must wear a lifejacket.
The boat and all the equipment must be safe.
Advice must be got regarding safety equipment, clothing, etc.
Everybody must be fit and well.

More than one person should know how to manage the boat.
Everybody must know how to swim and if possible lifesave.
A message must be left before setting out.
The "Captain" must be obeyed at all times.

21 If you see any person or any boat in difficulty at any time of the day or night, in the water or by the water.
If any person or boat is missing.
If you need any safety information before setting out on a trip, or if you are in the area for the first time.

22 Get expert advice before they go.
Always go with a group.
Make sure each person has their own safety equipment and correct clothing.
Leave a message before setting out.

23 Get all the advice you can before you go.
Take only safe equipment.
Choose a safe area.
Make a set of camp safety rules and see that they are kept.
Take extra care with stoves, matches, fires and fuel.
Bury glass and tins as soon as possible.
Keep all the general safety rules.
Take a first aid kit.
Keep all the hygiene rules.

Official Organisations

1 The National Health Service is made up of the following—
General Medical Service.
Hospital Service.
Local Health Service.
Mental Health Service.

2 The General Medical Service includes the following—
The Family Doctor—or group.
Dentist.
Ophthalmic service—eyes.
Pharmaceutical service—chemist.

3   Supplementary Benefit (cash payments) are available to
     people who are:
     Over 16.
     In need of help because of reasons of this kind;
     They are sick, unemployed, too old to work, or have to
     stay at home to look after young children.
     The amount of Supplementary Benefit people get depends
     on how much money they have coming in and how much
     they have to spend.

4   Public Health Inspectors deal with complaints about
     insanitary conditions in:
              Houses.
              Dairy farms.
              Premises where food is prepared or sold,
     as well as such things as smoke abatement, polluted water.

5   (a) Ante-natal clinics are the clinics that mothers attend
         before their babies are born.
         The mothers usually go each month and undergo such
         check-ups as the following:
                  Medical examinations.
                  Testing—blood, etc.
                  Being weighed.
         They are also given advice on diet, hygiene, etc.
     (b) After the baby is born the mother should attend the
         post-natal clinic (often called the Welfare Clinic).
         This is so that the doctor can be sure that things are
         going well for both mother and baby, e.g. the mother
         is advised about her own diet and the feeding of the
         baby. The doctor can also make sure that the mother
         is regaining her own health and energy.
     The clinics:
         The clinics must be in a convenient position for the
         mothers to get to.
         There must be a waiting room.
         The babies must be weighed.
         The mothers may be seen by the Health Visitor sometimes
         and the doctor at other times.
         Babies may be vaccinated and immunised in the clinic
         unless they are done by their family doctor.
         Mothers may also obtain Welfare foods for themselves and
         their babies, e.g. milk, vitamins, orange juice, etc.

6   Midwifery is part of the Health Service.
Midwives are State Registered nurses who have also passed examinations in midwifery.
Midwives attend ante-natal clinics and get to know the mothers.
The midwife is responsible for the delivery of normal births.
She sends for the doctor in an emergency.
After the baby is born the midwife visits the mother and baby for the next 14 days, after which the Health Visitor takes over.
The midwife may also visit the mother during her pregnancy and give her any advice she needs.

7   The Health Visitors are part of the Health Service.
Health Visitors are State Registered nurses with extra qualifications.
They attend ante-natal and post-natal clinics.
They have the care of the baby after it is 2 weeks old and of small children up to 5 years old.
The Health Visitor also keeps a check on the mother's health.
As well as looking after mothers and babies, Health Visitors do such work as:

> Supervising T.B. patients.
> Helping the aged.
> Teaching health.

They also get help from the various services available to people under the Health Service Act.
Infectious diseases have to be reported by the Health Visitor and she keeps a check on contacts.

8   District Nurses are State Registered nurses with extra qualifications.
They work among people in the people's own homes.
They work under the direction of the doctor.
District Nurses are able to get the free loan of any special equipment their patients may need.

9   The Home Help Service is part of the Local Government Health Service. The Home Help Service helps people in all cases of need, e.g. when people are sick, old, or when a mother has a new baby in hospital.
If people can afford to pay for the services of the Home Help they will be asked to pay according to their circumstances.

10 Almoners are employed in hospitals. They help patients in
many different ways.
If the patient has any difficulty which may stop him getting
better properly, the Almoner will help the patient.
E.g. the patient may be worrying about what is happening
at home. The Almoner would be able to get the help of a
Home Help for the family if necessary.
The Almoner is the link between the Hospital Service and
the various Social Services.
Sometimes an Almoner may also train Almoner students.

11 The School Health Service is usually the responsibility of the
School Medical Officer (he may also be the Medical Officer
of Health).
He has the help of School Nurses, who may visit the schools as
well as work in the school clinics.
All school children have regular medical and dental inspections,
as well as general cleanliness inspections, e.g. for hair, hands,
etc.

12 The Hospital Service provides the following:
Hospital accommodation.
Medical and nursing services.
Specialists.

Unofficial Organisations

1 The International Red Cross has branches all over the
world and the U.K. branch is called the British Red Cross
Society. Their aim is to help people in all kinds of need.
They train people in First Aid and Home Nursing, adults and
children.
They give help in hospitals with nursing and many other jobs.
When there are processions, football matches, etc., they go
on duty in case people faint or have accidents.
They also visit old people and take them "meals on wheels".

2 The Citizen's Advice Bureaux do all they can to help people
with all kinds of everyday problems, e.g. employment,
education, money, consumer complaints, housing,
marriage, etc.
There are branches in most cities and towns.

There is usually a general staff, who either help the person themselves, or put them in touch with professional people for advice on special matters, e.g., legal questions. Anybody can go to the C.A.B. and everything is kept confidential.

3 This Society exists to protect children from being hurt in any way by parents or anybody else.
They usually have to be told about the cases of cruelty.
They do not let anybody know who told them.
All kinds of cruelty should be reported, e.g. children beaten, left alone, not fed or clothed properly, not getting medical care if they are ill, etc.
The Society do all they can:
  To stop the child being ill treated.
  To help the parents if necessary.
  To bring really cruel people to justice.

4 The Order of St. John help people in many ways.
They train adults and children in First Aid.
They help in street accidents.
Wherever crowds gather for processions, meetings or to enjoy themselves, e.g. at the seaside, the St. John officers go on duty. They also help people in their own homes and in hospitals, e.g. taking people to hospital for treatment, taking "meals on wheels" to old people.

5 This organisation helps anybody who is in need.
They visit people in hospitals and prisons as well as look after their families.
They visit people in their homes and they take "meals on wheels" to old people.
They help all kinds of people who need clothes, etc.
They also help to collect clothes and anything else which may be needed by refugees.
As well as helping people in all these ways they also help in Civil Defence work.

6 This Society works in all kinds of ways to prevent accidents.
They do this in many ways, e.g.:
  Printing booklets and posters.
  Giving advice on safety to whoever wants it.
  Giving talks and lectures.

Children can belong to the "Tufty club" which is specially for them, to teach them road safety.

7   The R.S.P.C.A. work to protect all animals, including birds, from cruelty and from accidents.
The Society has clinics, shelters, and rest homes for animals. Whenever animals travel, e.g. to and from zoos or if they are being imported or exported to other countries, the officers of the R.S.P.C.A. will check up on the travelling conditions of the animals.

HOME

Planning and Caring for the Home

1   Houses—detached, semi-detached, terrace.
Bungalows and chalet bungalows.
Flats—purpose-built or houses converted.
Rooms.
Caravans, hotels, hostels, etc.

2   Go to several house agents.
Advertise and read advertisements.
Ask local authorities.
Ask around.

3   How much the rent is.
When you have to pay the rent.
If and when you have to pay the rates.
Is there an agreement to sign?

4   The Citizen's Advice Bureau.
A private solicitor.

5   Who does the repairs and decorating (inside and outside)?
Can you use the garden, to hang out washing, etc.?
How long a notice is there, on either side?
Are there any rules about children or animals?
What are the arrangements about heating, baths, etc.?

6   Will the house be big enough in a few years' time?
Heating and cooking method.
Are any fitments included in the house price?
Space for fuel if needed.
Is there plenty of light, size and position of the windows.
Number and size of cupboards.

7   When the house gets the sun and where.
Is the area safe for children?
Is there anything in the district you don't like?

Is it near the amenities your family needs, e.g. schools, shops, railway station, etc. ?
Are there any hilly roads to make shopping, etc., tiring ?

8 No damp proof course (or faulty one).
Damage to walls, roof, gutters, pipes, etc.
Not enough heat.
Poor ventilation.

9 A layer of waterproof material laid all round the top of the second layer of bricks before the rest of the wall is built up.

10 (a) It is decay caused by a fungus which draws water out of wood.
(b) By damp and poor ventilation.
(c) By the use of well-seasoned woods.
A dry, well-ventilated house.
Not painting on damp wood.
Keeping a check on all the wood parts of the house.

11 Damp rot occurs when wood gets wet and doesn't dry out.

12 By preventing wood getting wet, e.g. mend leaky pipes.

13 Solid fuel, e.g. coal.
Gas.
Electricity.
Oil.

14 Only use the amount of heat you need.
Don't leave doors open in separately heated rooms.
Put a thermometer in each room.
Insulate the house well.

15 Keeping the cold out and the heat in.

16 Deal with the house itself first, e.g. use foam or rubber strips to make doors and windows fit.
Mend any gaps in floors, round windows and doors.
Buy warm furnishings such as thick curtains, carpets and underlays, etc.
Buy insulating material for walls and roof, e.g. rolls of glass wool, loose filling, polystyrene, etc.
Wrap up water pipes and tanks.

17 Order fuel in the summer—get it delivered early.
Check fireplaces, heaters and chimneys.
Mend any leaky taps.
Insulate the house well.

18 Have windows in the best positions, if possible.
Use glass panels in doors to give extra light in dark passages.
Place mirrors carefully to reflect light.
Keep all windows and glass clean.
Don't block out too much light with the curtaining.

19 Central lighting—not suitable for all rooms.
Strip lighting—useful if it doesn't throw shadows.
Separate lamps and spot lights—good for lighting
particular parts of a room.

20 A well-ventilated house is a house where stale air is being
continually taken out and fresh air brought in, without
draughts.

21 By opening windows and doors.
Having small ventilators fitted in windows.
Air bricks and gratings in walls.
Extractor fans in walls or windows.

22 Fit new washers to dripping taps.
Never leave taps running.
Do not leave hoses on, unattended, in the garden.
Keeping a check on overflow pipes for trouble.

23 Do not leave taps dripping in cold weather.
Pour salt down sinks at night.
Make sure all pipes are well lagged (the water tanks too).
Do not leave bathroom and lavatory windows wide open on
cold nights.

24 Try to get somebody to come in to put some heat on in the
house. Before you go, turn off the water and empty all the
taps.

25 The central heating system.
Some cooking ranges.
Separate water heaters, e.g. immersion heaters, gas heaters
over sinks and baths.

26 Don't waste the water by leaving the taps running.
Don't leave immersion heater cupboard doors open.
Keep cistern jackets and pipe laggings in position and in
good repair.
Don't leave immersion heaters on unnecessarily.

27 No, because it might blow up.

28 Too much grease.
Tea leaves.
Food waste, including vegetable peelings
Bits of dishcloth.
Flower petals and leaves.

29 (a) Press a sink plunger down and up over the plug hole.
If this doesn't work:
(b) Turn off the water.
Put a bucket under the sink.
Undo the large screw.
Push a piece of cane or wire up the pipe.
When the pipe is cleared replace the screw.

30 Too much or too thick toilet paper.
Bits of cloth and some sanitary towels.
Kitchen waste.
Emptying paper baskets into it.

31 Don't let them get blocked.
Keep them cleared out (papers, leaves, etc.).
Pour boiling water down and brush well every so often.
Call a plumber or inform the Sanitary department if you
think there is something seriously wrong.

32 Keep them clear of leaves and other rubbish.
Make sure they are fixed securely.
Keep the cages on the tops of pipes in repair and in position.
Keep them painted.

33 It should be suitable for the purpose, e.g. washable for
kitchens, lead-free if there are children in the house.
Should be hard wearing.
Any other special points, e.g. heatproof, insect-repellent,
non-drip, etc.

34 Wallpaper, wood panelling.
Materials such as hessian and linen,
Tiles.
Vinyl.
Paint.
Distemper.

35 Clear out all pictures, ornaments, etc.
Take down the curtains.
Roll up carpets and rugs.
Take curtains, carpets, rugs, small furniture into another
room.
Push large furniture into the middle of the room and cover.
Cover the floor with paper or large sheets of polythene.

36 Modern, Whitewood, Kits to assemble, Homemade.
Old, Very old (Antique), copies of antique furniture.
Furniture from other countries.

37 Lino—best should be used in kitchens and other rooms
where it will get heavy wear.
Vinyl—sheets and tiles, useful in any room but may be
slippery when wet.
Cork—warm and quiet—needs to be sealed if used in
bathrooms.
Rubber—sheets and tiles—useful for bathrooms and halls—
needs careful cleaning.
Hardboard—useful anywhere.
Quarry tiles—cold but hard wearing—used mostly in
kitchens, need rugs.
Rush matting—useful anywhere—must be kept in good repair.
Carpets and rugs—useful anywhere, warm and quiet, must
be kept in good repair.

38 What is it made of?
Is it suitable for the room you want it for?
How long can you expect it to last?
How can it be cleaned?
What widths is it sold in?
Special points such as, is it mothproof, will it burn easily, etc.

39 They are the names which describe the weave of the carpet.
There are several grades.

40 They protect the carpet.
They make the room warmer.
They deaden sound.

41 The size of the windows.
How long the curtains are to be.
How full you want them.
Whether they are to be lined. In this case lining material
must be bought too.

42 Price.
Suitability for the room they are to go in.
Thickness of the material for your purpose, e.g. for winter, to
be draped, etc.
Is it washable or must it be dry cleaned?
Is it non-flam material?
Is it mothproof?

43 Is it strong, warm, non-flammable, slippery, waterproof?
Will it match the rest of the room?

44 It should be safe.
Warm.
Airy but not draughty.
Easy to clean.
Furnished and planned so that it can "grow" with the child.

45 It should be safe.
Warm.
Airy but not draughty.
Restful, cheerful and comfortable.
Not too far away from the rest of the family rooms.
Easy in every way for the old person to manage.
Providing space for at least some of their own things.

46 Read the directions.
Don't waste.
Keep lids on when not in use.
Use the mildest cleaner for the job, e.g. baths don't always
need scouring powders—cleaning pastes are often more
suitable.
Take note of any new cleaners; they may do the job you
want done better than the one you usually use.

47 Pick up anything which may damage the vacuum cleaner, e.g. pins, hairclips, etc.
Treat the cleaner carefully.
Be careful with the flex and plug.
Keep the cleaner clean and in good repair.
Empty the bag regularly.
Store cleaner and attachments tidily in a clean place.

48 Keep them clean. Wash yellow dusters on their own.
Boil tea towels and dishcloths. Don't forget the oven cloth.
Make sure the cloths are dry before putting them away.
Store in a clean, dry place.
Don't leave damp cloths on top of scouring tins.
Use up old rags for the dirtiest work and then throw them away.
Use paper towels when these are convenient.

49 Keep them clean—dry well after washing.
Use the right brush or broom for the job.
Store carefully, best to hang them up.

50 Follow directions.
Usual method—
Wash in hot water with a little detergent.
Do not use scourers or cleaning powders.
Do not scratch with knives, etc.
Rinse in clean hot water.
Dry and put away.

51 Put to soak if necessary, e.g. milk pans and burnt pans.
If badly stained, use scouring powder, pads or nylon scourers.
Rinse in hot water.
Dry well, especially tin.

52 Cover the table with newspaper.
Use the correct cleaner.
Follow directions carefully.
Copper and brass are sometimes lacquered to save cleaning.

53 Wash in hot water.
Dry and polish.
If badly stained, get a special cleaner for chromium and use according to the directions.

54 Wash in hot water with a little detergent.
Rinse in hot water.
Dry and put away.
If badly stained use a special cleaner according to the
directions.

55 Wash at once after use.
If stained—rub with cork dipped in scouring powder.
Rinse and dry well.

56 Cover the table with newspaper.
Use the correct cleaner.
Follow the directions carefully.
Wash cutlery, dry well and put away carefully.
Treat silver carefully because it scratches easily.

57 Cooking equipment—Scrape off scraps with a palette knife.
All white wood—
Wipe with a damp cloth.
Scrub if necessary (the way of the grain).
Rinse with clean water.
Dry as much as possible.
Don't dry by a fierce heat.

58 Dust with a soft cloth.
Wash with warm water and a little detergent.
Rinse with clean water.
Rub dry.
Stubborn marks may need a little cleaning paste on the
cloth.

59 Dust with a soft duster.
Rub up with another duster.
Use a little polish, according to the directions, sometimes.
Use a soft brush for narrow ledges and crevices on furniture.

60 There are several kinds of beetle which attack wood.
The female lays her eggs in the wood.
The grubs eat their way out and make little holes in the
wood.
If this is not noticed the wood may be weakened until it
collapses.

To prevent:
Use ready protected woods.
Use wax polish on furniture. This discourages the female laying her eggs. (Put polish on back of wood too.)
To treat:
Use a special substance which may be bought for the job.
Call in an expert.
Homes can be insured against woodworm, which is the name often given to the damage done by furniture beetles.

61 Wipe up spills at once.
Use a little detergent or special cleaner for stubborn stains. (Best to test the cleaner first on a part of the furniture which won't show.)
Use a vacuum cleaner or furniture brush to remove dust.
Loose cushions must be removed and cleaned too.
Plastic covers usually only need a wipe with a damp cloth and are then rubbed dry.

62 Use a chamois leather and warm water to wash.
Dry with a dry chamois leather or old linen cloth.
Use a special window cleaner according to the directions.

63 Take it down carefully.
Dust back and front with a soft duster.
Check the cords.
Clean the glass, taking care not to use too much water.
Rehang straight.
Valuable pictures should be cleaned professionally.

64 Spills should be wiped up at once.
Any stubborn stains may need a commercial cleaner. Use according to directions. Usually better to get advice from the carpet manufacturer if possible.
Use the carpet sweeper daily, especially after meals.
Vacuum when necessary.
Shampoo the carpet if really dirty, or have it cleaned.

65 Sweep or mop when necessary.
Wipe up spills at once.
Wash when necessary. Rinse with clean water.
Dry well.
Polish if required, using a non-slip polish.

66 Sweep or mop when necessary.
Wipe up spills at once.
Wash with warm water and a little detergent.
Rinse with clean water.
Dry well.
Bad stains may need to be rubbed with a little cleaning
paste on a damp cloth.

67 Sweep or mop when necessary.
Wipe up spills at once.
Wash with special liquid from the manufacturers.
Polish when necessary with special polish.

68 Wash or mop with warm water and a little detergent. Rinse.
Dry well.

69 Take everything out.
Wipe out with warm water and a little detergent.
Rinse with clean water and dry well.
Leave open to dry or leave by a current of air (not near
a fire).
Replace things tidily.

70 Collect cleaning equipment and materials.
Vacuum or brush where necessary.
Clean windows and mirrors.
Wash off any marks on paintwork.
Polish furniture and floor if necessary.
Dust everywhere.
Replace everything.
You may need to vacuum the carpet here and there to finish.

71 Clear away food.
Wipe larder shelves if necessary.
Clear the table.
Wash up and put the milk bottles out.
Wipe the stove.
Wipe any other surfaces which may need it.
Tidy up.
Sweep or mop floor.

72 Open the window.
Clear grate and light fire. Put up guard.

Tidy up.
Sweep the carpet with the carpet sweeper. (Mop any surround.)
Dust.

73 Make the bed, which should already have been left to air.
Tidy the room.
Sweep the floor with the carpet sweeper or mop.
Dust.

74 Open the window.
Tidy the room.
Wipe round bath and washbasin.
Mop the floor.

75 Check that the window is open.
Flush, brush and flush the pan.
Dust.
Check the toilet paper.

76 Only put clean jars, etc., in.
Put lids on jars and close packet tops before putting them in the larder.
Wipe up any spills as soon as you see them.
Check all perishable food every day.
Don't put hot foods in—let them cool first.

77 Turn off the gas taps.
Take any pans off the cooker (plates and plate rack too if there is one).
Put grill pan, burners and shelves in the sink to soak.
Clean the oven.
Wash and dry enamel parts.
Clean burners, shelves, etc.
Replace burners and test for lighting.
Replace rest of parts.
Rub up chromium parts.
Wipe the floor and clean the sink.

78 Turn off the main switch.
Take any pans off the cooker.
Prepare hot water and detergent in the sink.

Take the trays from under the hotplates (if they are movable).
Put them in the sink to soak.
Put the grill pans and oven shelves into the sink.
Clean the oven.
Wash and dry enamel parts.
Wipe and polish any chromium parts.
Replace all the parts of the cooker.
Wipe the floor and clean the sink.

79 Wipe up any spills at once.
Wipe bottles before putting them in.
Only put fresh food into the refrigerator.
Check the contents regularly.
If gas or electricity has been turned off, make sure the refrigerator is working properly when the current or gas is on again.
Make sure all food is wrapped or covered.
If the refrigerator is to be left empty for any length of time leave the door open.

80 Don't put hot food in.
Don't pack food too tightly.
Don't leave the door open.
Don't use the refrigerator as a larder.
If the electricity or gas is to be off for a long time don't leave food in the refrigerator.
Never put animals' food in the refrigerator—the family can be poisoned.
Don't let too much ice collect on the cooling unit.

81 Make sure everything is clean and shining.
Set the table neatly.
Make sure the condiment set is filled.
Check the table before the meal is started to make sure nothing is forgotten.

82 Use a tray or trolley to put the things on.
Clear the food off the table first and put it away.
Clear away the cutlery, plates, etc.
Remove cloths, mats, etc.
Dust any crumbs off the table.
Sweep the floor if necessary.
Replace chairs.

83 Glass.
Cutlery.
Crockery—cleanest things first.
Cooking utensils.
Rinse everything before putting in drying racks or drying
with a teatowel.

84 Collect everything you want.
Turn the carpet or rug back and put newspaper on the
floor.
Brush the soot from the back of the fireplace.
Rake out the ashes and put them in the bucket—put a few
cinders back into the grate.
Lay screwed-up paper on the cinders.
Put on the wood and coal.
Brush and wash the hearth.
Fold up the paper from the floor.
Light the fire and put the guard up.
Take the ashes, etc., outside.
Replace the carpet or rug.

85 (a) Drain wet rubbish.
Don't put broken glass or tins in the pedal bin if there
are children in the house.
Empty pedal bin often.
Wash and dry.
Put clean paper in, or plastic bag (bag only if there are
no small children about).
(b) Wrap rubbish in newspaper before putting it in the
bin.
Scrub out the bin regularly.
Leave upside down to dry.
Put newspaper and powdered disinfectant in the
bottom.
Keep the lid of the dustbin on.

86 Don't cook—use raw foods for all or part of the meal.
Share the cooking—get somebody to help you.
Plan ahead so that one day's cooking will help towards the
next day's.
Use quick methods, e.g. grating, parboiling, small sizes for
pies, etc.
Use convenience foods for part of the meals.

87 Plan the work.
Work tidily and cleanly.
Make it easy with time-saving equipment and materials.
Don't do it—get help, send jobs out, etc.

88 Divide the day into blocks of time.
Make a note of rush times.
Work out the best time for the housewife to get some rest.
Share out the jobs for everybody.

89 For health care, e.g. extra rest.
For "beauty" treatments.
Getting clothes.
Learning—hobbies, etc.
Spending time for going out with family, friends, etc.
Going to church or just thinking about things.

90 Keep up with her girl friends.
Be friendly to everybody.
Do jobs like poppy selling, savings collecting, etc.
Join a club or some kind of group, e.g. flower arranging.
Keep up with the family.
Entertain as much as possible—if only for coffee.
Go out as much as possible.
See the doctor if these things don't work.

91 Regularity—mealtimes, etc.
Have at least one clock showing correct time.
Plenty of time—to get ready for work, etc.
Share the jobs.
Keep everything in the right place.
Get odd repair jobs done at once.
Have the right tools for odd jobs.
Keep spares of things that cause inconvenience if they
run out.
Have plenty of change for small fares, lunch money, etc.
Cut out unnecessary noise.

Safety–General

1 That the whole building should be safely constructed.
That every part should be made of safe materials.

2 Use louvre type windows if possible.
Keep them in good repair.
Fix vertical bars to prevent children falling out.
Board or fence in balconies so that little children can't get through or climb over.

3 Use armour plate glass.
Fix guard rails across.

4 Fix a hand rail on the wall side.
Put gates at the top and the bottom of the stairs.
Board in banisters if they are too far apart.

5 On staircases, especially if they turn corners.
In any dark corners of the house.
In deep cupboards.
At the front and the back doors if there are steps.
Wherever people do jobs that need a good light.

6 The materials the thing is made of should be safe.
The materials should be of a good quality.
The article should be well designed and well made.
The article should be easily managed by the person who has to use it, e.g. the right size and weight.

7 The British Standards Institution.
The Design Council.
The Consumers' Association.
The Government.

8 Kite mark.

9 It should be strongly made.
It must stand firm, yet move easily.
It should have no rough or sharp edges.
It must work properly, e.g. drawers open and shut easily.
It must be the right size, height, etc.
Look for B.S.I. numbers, Kite mark, etc.

10 B.S.I. numbers and Electric Approval Mark.
Double insulation and safety cut-outs.
If the article comes from a foreign country, get it checked by a qualified electrician.

11 Look for the Gas Board's safety sign.
Ask about any safety parts which may be fitted.

12 Look for the B.S.I. numbers and the Kite mark and the mark
of the Oil Appliance Manufacturers' Association.
Ask about non-spill oil cans and any other safety points.

13 Things made of china and glass should be safe in the
following ways:
They should be well balanced and easy to hold.
They should stack well if necessary.
If children are to use the things they must be as unbreakable
as possible.
Teapots should have well-fitting lids and pour properly.

14 Knives should be sharp enough and have well-fixed handles.
Carving-knives must have strong guards.
Forks should be well balanced and have no sharp points.

15 The lids should fit well.
The utensils should be well balanced and easy to hold.
The handles shouldn't get too hot to hold and shouldn't be
slippery.

16 Wherever possible look for "non-flare" materials, e.g. fibre
glass for curtains.
Materials should be strong enough for the job.

17 Everything for children should be as safe as possible.
Materials should be "non-flare" for as many clothes, bedclothes and toys as possible.
All articles should be checked for safety, e.g. pillows, safety
straps, etc.

18 Fireguards—Look for B.S.I. numbers. Make sure the model
can be fixed firmly to your fireplace.
Plastics—look for B.S.I. numbers.
Christmas decorations—Choose the ones which are "non-
flare" and "melt-proof", or make your own with fireproof
materials.
Hearthrugs—"non-flare" and non-slip.
Also materials which won't fray, causing falls.

Bedside lamps—Must have a firm base. Also "non-flare" shades.

Bolts for bathroom doors—The safest ones are those which open from both sides.

19 Electric, gas and oil appliances.
Cutting articles.
Anything which uses very hot water.

20 Don't wear loose, flowing clothes which can easily catch on doors or knock pans off stoves.
Don't wear clothes which are torn or worn so badly as to be dangerous.
Wear well-fastened shoes with flat heels.

21 Equipment should always be used properly.
It should always be used for the correct purpose.
All equipment should be kept in good repair.
Regular checking is very important.
Equipment should be stored carefully when not in use.

22 Strong steps with non-slip treads are best.
Long-handled brushes are useful for some jobs, as the housewife need not climb on to anything.

23 When not in use they must be stored in a place that small children really cannot get at.
When they are being used they must not be left where a child can touch them.
As far as possible lids should be kept firmly fixed when not in use.
All cleaning materials must be used exactly according to the directions, e.g. don't use flammable cleaners near naked lights.
Labels should be kept clean and not torn.
All cleaning materials must be kept in their own containers.
When containers are empty it is safer to throw them away.

24 The following things must all be well wrapped and put into the dustbin.
Any containers which have had dangerous substances in them.
Anything sharp.

Old food.
Anything which may be dangerous should not be left in the
house for any length of time.

25 Keep all sharp and pointed things locked up when not in
use. Be very careful if you have to use sharp things when
children are near.
Never let small children be near the sewing machine when
you are using it.
Don't stick pins and needles into dress fronts, arms of
chairs or mattresses "just for a minute".
Keep all the electric safety rules when using electric sewing
machines.
When using hand machines never let somebody else turn
the handle.
Keep machine oil locked up.

26 (a) They can cause people to fall by: Sitting on the stairs.
Getting under foot.
(b) They can cause fires by: Knocking over oil stoves.
Tossing paper about.

27 Always keep dogs on the lead where there is traffic on the
road.
Teach them "kerb drill".
Don't let small children hold big dogs.
Don't exercise them whilst you are riding a bicycle.
Teach them not to jump up at people.
Keep them tied up when in cars (have a little window open
with a safety guard if you leave them in the car on a hot
day).

28 Strong ladders and steps.
Strong tools.
The right tools for the job.
Safe electrical equipment.
Scaffolding and lifting equipment for big jobs (can be
borrowed).

29 Use them carefully.
Store them carefully.
Keep them in good repair.

30 All materials should be checked to find out if they are:
inflammable, poisonous, explosive, or dangerous if breathed
in.

31 Worn floor or stair coverings.
Broken banisters or stairs.
Windows—broken sash cords, loose fastenings, etc.
Ceilings and walls—cracks.
Fireplaces—broken fire backs and hearths.
Dry rot and furniture beetle damage.
Any gas, electric or oil appliance which is not working
properly.

32 Loose tiles.
Broken or loose pipes and gutterings.
Damaged chimneys and chimney stacks.
Stopped-up flue outlets.
Broken gates and fences.
Broken steps and paths.

33 Poisoning (coal gas), explosion, fire.

34 Turn off the gas at the mains if you can.
Open the window.
Telephone the Gas Board.
If the smell of gas is very strong as you enter the house,
don't go in, go and telephone the Gas Board instead.

35 Never look for a gas leak with a naked light.
Don't do any jobs on gas appliances—get the gas man to
do them.
Have your equipment checked yearly.
Use all appliances carefully.
Make sure large equipment is properly vented.
Test all the family to make sure they can smell properly.
Make sure somebody knows how to, and can, turn the gas
off at the main.

36 Check the pilot light often to make sure it is alight.
Make sure the water heater is turned off before you get
into the bath.
Always have the window open a little.
Keep the flue clear.

37 All the family must be told how to use electrical equipment safely and the dangers of not doing so.
Installations and repairs should be done by a qualified electrician.
Appliances must only be used for the correct purpose.
The installation and appliances should be checked at regular intervals. The Electricity Board will advise.
If an appliance doesn't seem to be working properly, it should not be used until a qualified electrician has checked it.
Take extra care when using water and electrical appliances at the same time.

38 Flexes should be as short as practicable.
They are dangerous if they are: frayed, knotted, run under mats or badly repaired.
Flexes should be fitted to appliances by qualified electricians only.
Christmas decorations, etc., must never be pinned to flexes.

39 Overloading means making electric wires carry too much current.

40 By not running power appliances from the light.
By not running too many appliances from the same power point.
By not using too many appliances in the house at the same time.
Have enough power points.
Find out from a qualified electrician the total load your installation can carry.

41 No. The only kind of electric heater which is safe is a wall heater fitted by a qualified electrician.

42 Keep it clear of dangerous rubbish.
Make sure toys and garden equipment are put away after use.
Don't leave milk bottles on the step if there are small children about.
Make sure there is safe storage space for poisonous garden sprays, etc., and mowers and other garden tools.

43 All repair jobs to gates and fences.
Repairs to steps and paths.
Paths and steps must be cleared of snow as quickly as possible.
Grass should be kept short where there are small children.
(Easier to see anything lying about.)

44 All equipment must be used with care, especially if it is powered by electricity.
Equipment must be safe and kept in good repair.
Children must not be allowed to use tools until they have been properly taught and are old enough to do so.

45 If they are used as play sheds they must:
Not contain any dangerous garden substance or equipment.
Be properly ventilated.
Be as fireproof as possible. Children must not be allowed to take matches or anything which could start a fire into the shed.
Be inspected regularly by parents.

46 Make sure all water, ponds, pools, water-butts, etc., are covered if there are small children in the house.
Children must only be allowed to play in pools, even little ones, if an adult is present.
If you have a swimming pool get all the safety equipment too.

47 By children playing with matches, etc.
Through unguarded fires.
By smokers.
When gas, electricity and oil are not used properly.
By curtains blowing on to stoves and candles.
By unswept chimneys.
By badly used or stored inflammable substances.
By glass left lying about and catching the sun's rays.

48 Burning, suffocating, poisoning.
Flames, hot air and smoke all kill people.

49 Use fuels carefully.
Make the house as safe from fire as possible.
Make outside buildings safe from fire too.

Cook with care, especially when using fat.
Never leave inflammable things near fires.
Buy everything you can "safe from fire".
Teach children fire safety.
Make sure fires can't start when you are out.
Stand portable fires on something which won't burn.
Never bring petrol into the house.

50 Don't use petrol or paraffin to light the fire.
Don't use inflammable things to draw up the fire.
Don't leave inflammable things near a fire.
Never leave a fire without the guard up.
Don't put the ashes in paper or cardboard boxes.
Take care when using gas pokers.

51 Don't make the fire up too near bedtime.
Never leave a blazing fire—bank it down with damp slack.
Make sure the guard is fixed.
Roll back the rug.
Shut the window and the door.

52 Don't put too much fuel on.
Don't throw paper on to the fire.
Don't use wood on top of the fire.

53 Have them swept regularly.
Always keep the lower part of the chimney free from soot.
If the chimney keeps smoking, get the sweep or a builder to
check up for you.

54 Mirrors, clocks, papers, Christmas cards, children's toys.

55 Put them on a fireproof base where they stand firm and are
out of draughts, and people don't have to keep passing them.
Make sure there is nothing inflammable nearby.
Never fill them indoors.
Use a safety can—wipe up any oil on the stove, wipe
your hands.
Never light an oil stove if you are smoking.
Don't let children carry them.
Keep them clean and in good repair.
Always use the correct fuel.
Don't put fuel in when the stove is alight.

56 Cleaning substances.
Garages (petrol).
Paraffin oil.
Turpentine, varnishes, paint strippers.
Methylated spirits, lighter fuel.
Nail varnish, hair sprays, perfume.

57 Don't smoke near inflammable things.
Obey all non-smoking notices.
Make sure matches and cigarette ends are really out, then put them in the ash tray, or grind them out completely.
Don't flick hot ash about.
Pipes must not be knocked out where they can set fire to something, and never left about unless they are really out.

58 When people are alone.
In cars, ash trays must always be used.
Outdoors on hot days where grass, etc., is very dry.
Smoking in bed should never be done.

59 Paper, wood, sawdust, dust, fluff.
Old paint and varnish tins.
Oily rags.
Old furniture, mattresses, etc.

60 Empty aerosols.
Empty tubes with the lid on.
Anything greasy.
Dust and old rags.
Paper, materials, etc.

61 Never light fires near the house, sheds, fences or dry grass.
Don't throw inflammable things on bonfires.
If you have to leave a bonfire damp it down first.
Put bonfires right out at night.

62 Don't put them too near the heat.
Don't leave them near the heat too long.
Use safe airing equipment.

63 (a) Never leave it on the mantelpiece or near any fire.
(b) Store in a cool place.

(c) Keep in a cold place. It is safer never to keep any petrol in the house.

(d) Don't leave them near fires or where the sun can shine on them.

(e) Store them in a cool place.

64 Read all labels and directions carefully. Some of the things used to do these hobbies are inflammable, e.g. some chemicals, some liquids used in photography, some adhesives. Consequently special care should be taken in using and storing them.

65 In winter.
If you have to leave the house at any time.
Bedtime.
Party times.

66 Guard all fires.
Fix any candles really well or don't use them.
Clear paper things away as soon as possible.
If children come in fancy dress take extra care, e.g. don't let them go into the kitchen.

67 Never put decorations near fires, light bulbs, candles, or in the kitchen.
Turn electric decorations off if you go out and when you go to bed.
Don't put candles on trees.
Don't put the tree near a fire.
Get rid of wrappings as soon as possible. Don't let people hang them up as extra decorations.

68 (a) Little children—must not be allowed to touch fireworks.
They should not be allowed to go near the bonfire either.
They are safer watching through a window.

(b) Fireworks—directions must be read before lighting them.
They must never be let off indoors.
They must not be put in pockets.
They must not be put on mantelpieces or in kitchens.
They must never be "home-made".

(c) Bonfires—All the rules for garden bonfires must be kept.
The box of fireworks must be kept well away from the bonfire.

F

69 (a) Don't leave fires on unless they are very well guarded.
It is usually thought safer not to leave oil stoves on
at all.
Never leave a child alone in the house with any fire on.
If you go out for the day don't leave any fire on.

   (b) When you go away—
Switch off gas and electricity at the mains.
Turn off all gas taps and pilot lights.
Make sure open fires and boilers are really out.
Close the inside doors.
Don't smoke when you do your last check-up.

70 Check all the heating equipment, including electric blankets.
Have the chimney swept.
Clear out all inflammable rubbish.

71 Check that the fire is safe—banked down, rug rolled back,
guard up.
Unplug electric appliances, except refrigerator and clock for
instance.
Make sure portable fires are really out.
Check ashtrays, look around the floor, under cushions, on
the mantelpiece, to make sure no cigarette ends or pipes are
left about.
Check that all parts of the cooker are off.
Close all the doors and windows.

72 Everybody out at once.

73 Fires can't spread so quickly if as many things as possible in
the house are made of non-flam materials.
Fires won't spread so much if they are not fanned, i.e. if
doors and windows are closed.

74 For escaping:—
Fire escape stairs and ladders.
Cradles for letting down children, old people or invalids.
Ropes, fluffy and webbing types.
Fire extinguisher—Look for safety mark—get advice on
which to get from the fire brigade.
Fire blanket or old army blanket.
Buckets of water, sand or earth.
Safer to have these things upstairs and downstairs.

75 The Fire Protection Association.

76 Whenever a fire starts the rule is, Send for the Fire Brigade.

77 By dialling 999 in most areas.
The caller should try to be calm.
He must be able to answer the operator's questions, as to where the fire is etc.

78 Yes, because they can spread and cause the whole house to burn.

79 Put the flames out first by laying the person on the floor and rolling him in a rug.
Call the Fire Brigade and Ambulance. (This can be done earlier if there is somebody else at hand.)

80 No. You should feel the door first.
If it is cold, lean against it and open it a little way to look. If it is warm, it means there is a lot of heat and smoke behind it. Call the Fire Brigade.

81 Turn off the heat.
Smother the pan with a damp (not wet) cloth or sand, earth or a fire blanket. If the fire gets out of control call the Fire Brigade.

82 Yes, because then there will be no panic and everybody will get out safely. If possible work out two routes in case the first one is blocked.

83 Yes, and always properly conducted by a parent.

84 Get a refill at once. Better still to keep one in hand.

85 Fit good locks to all windows, doors and skylights.
Lock all windows, doors and skylights when you go out.
Take care who you let in.

86 Safest never to let any stranger into your home if you are not satisfied about them.
Best to have a safety chain on the door so that you don't need to open the door too wide if strangers call.

If you are alone in the house it's better to look through the
window or call through the door, if somebody comes when
you are not expecting anybody.
If a caller does seem odd it's best to let the police know
straight away.
Children should be told never to open the door at all to
anybody, if they have to be alone in the house for any
reason.

87 Never leave a front or back door open if you can't see it,
even if you are in the garden.
Don't leave the outside doors unlocked if you are just
popping in next door for a minute.
Don't leave outside doors open if you are doing noisy jobs
indoors or watching television, or having a party, which
may mean you wouldn't hear a stranger walk in. All windows
should either be closed at night or fitted with a window
lock so that they can be fixed open as far as you want them
open, but can't be pushed open further.

88 Report to the police any suspicious happening or persons
hanging around other people's houses.

89 Cancel papers, milk, etc.
Put your valuables in the bank.
Ask a neighbour to keep an eye on your house.
Let the police know.

90 There are many things which can be bought to protect
houses from burglars. Here are some of them: Safety chains
and door optics for doors. Safety locks for the opening side
as well as the hinge side for doors.
For windows there are special locks, bolts and grilles for all
types of window.
Several types of alarm systems can be bought, as well as
dogs. The police will advise people on the best things to
buy for protecting their homes from burglars.

91 The safest place is in the bank.

92 Never leave your purse in an open shopping bag.
Don't put your handbag, purse, or cheque book down anywhere even for a second.

Make sure the clasp on your handbag is strong.

Don't give your handbag or any other valuable thing to small children to hold.

Don't tell everybody if you are carrying a lot of money or any other valuable thing.

Don't take more money than you need when you go shopping.

93 Never leave cars in badly lit places if you can help it.

Get anti-theft devices fitted to the car.

Don't forget to take out the ignition key, close the windows and lock the doors before you leave the car, even outside your own front door.

94 They will give people advice on all kinds of safety-from-crime points.

They will keep an eye on your house if you have to go away.

They will follow up any suspicious happenings or people if you report the matter.

Kitchens

1 A well-planned kitchen should be:

Safe.

Easy to clean.

Pleasant to work in.

Convenient to work in.

2 All working surfaces should be the correct height. This includes sinks and cookers.

Large equipment should be arranged for easy working sequences.

Heavy utensils should be stored where they can be easily got at.

All utensils should be stored near to where they are usually used.

3 The kind of fuel it uses.

The cost.

The size—

Will it fit the kitchen? Will it be large enough for the number of people it is to be used for to start with, and later?

Has it enough storage space for plates and cooking utensils.
Is the grill large enough for the amount of grilling to be done?
Is the oven large enough and are there enough burners or hot plates?
Cleaning—will it be easy to clean?
Construction—is it strongly made, are there any sharp edges?
Will pans tip over easily?

4   Always use the cooker correctly, safely and economically.
Keep it clean, oven, burners, etc.
Make full use of any special features it may have, e.g. automatic timing, etc.
If it seems at all faulty get it checked at once.

5   The price you can pay.
A suitable size for the work you intend it for and the space it has to go into.
Will you need two draining boards or will one be enough (right or left handed)?
What material do you want, e.g. plastic, porcelain, stainless steel?

6   Don't stop up the outlets with rubbish.
Keep it clean—use the correct cleaner.
Use plastic bowls when necessary.

7   Price.
Type—Do you want it silent?—choose an absorption type.
Fuel—gas or electric?
Size—you need one which is large enough for your kind of catering, e.g. do you buy lots of perishable foods? Do you have lots of parties?
Will it be large enough for later on?
Construction—look for easy control, well-fitting shelves, self-cleaning features, etc.

8   Use the refrigerator according to the directions given with it.
Keep it clean and tidy at all times.
Use it to save time, e.g. by preparing food in advance.
Use it to save money, e.g. by buying larger quantities when food is cheap.

Don't forget food, especially left-overs and food at the back of the refrigerator.

9 The most suitable material for your requirements—choose from: aluminium, enamel, stainless steel, copper, etc. Buy the type suitable for your cooker, whether it's gas or electric. Buy the correct size. If the saucepans are too big, fuel is wasted, on the other hand they must be large enough for present use and for later on. It's usually best to get one of each size and then get more later.
Look for safety points.
Look for easy-care points.

10 They must be strongly made and have no sharp edges. Materials include: tin, aluminium, coated and non-coated. Cake tins are useful if they have a loose bottom.
Try to buy tins in the sizes you want them.

11 Knives—must cut well and be well made.
Forks—the points should not be too sharp. It should be easy to clean between the prongs.
Spoons—buy all the sizes you need.
Scissors—must cut well and have handles which are not sharp.
All cutlery should be easy to handle.

12 Look for the ones which are easy to hold.
Materials include: oven-proof glass, earthenware, vitreous enamel. Other points to look for include: are they easy to clean? Will they break easily? Will they look nice on the table if you want to put them on the table?

13 Points to look for include: the right size for your purpose, good balance, stackability.
Materials—glass, earthenware, nylon, plastic and stainless steel.

14 Always buy the safest.
Buy well-made things.
Use them carefully and always for the right purpose.
Clean them properly.
Store carefully.

Kitchen Hygiene

1   Easy-to-clean coverings in good repair, e.g. Vinyl, well-fitting tiles and good quality lino.

2   By being covered with smooth easy-clean material, e.g. tiles, washable wallpaper or gloss paint.
    By being regularly cleaned down.

3   Any absorbent covering in good repair,
    e.g. non-washable distemper redecorated about every six months.

4   Because insects breed in dark corners.
    Because dirt and dust can be seen if the light is good, and then cleaned up.

5   By keeping the kitchen well ventilated.

6   Clean regularly.
    Buy everything which will clean easily.
    Buy as many things as possible to make cleaning easy.
    Throw rubbish away as soon as possible.

7   Smooth hard surfaces are best, e.g. Formica, metal, gloss paint.

8   Slots in sliding doors on cupboards.
    The cupboard under the sink and the sink pipes.
    Sink outlets.
    The cutlery drawer.
    The tops of tiles on half tiled walls.

9   Never leave scraps of food lying about on the floor, etc.
    Always put food away when finished with.
    Keep the floors and walls in good repair.
    Check the drains often and keep them very clean.
    Keep an eye open for signs of pests, e.g. droppings, greasy marks on walls, teeth marks on food.
    Use pest killers at the first signs that there are pests around.
    Inform the Public Health Department if you suspect that there are rats about.

10 By bacteria from people—from the nose, throat, bowels, cuts and sores.
By animals—domestic, and rats, mice, etc.
Dirt and dust.
Infected food and water.

11 The shop—must be clean.
The assistants—must be clean with no dirty habits, e.g. licking fingers.
The food—cooked meats must not be handled by assistants who serve fresh meat unless they wash their hands first.
Frozen food must not be left around the shop before being packed into the refrigerator.
The refrigerator must not be overfilled.
Date stamps must be checked before you buy date-stamped food.
All food must be in a clean and fresh condition.
The shopper—must behave in a hygienic manner, not sneezing or breathing over food, not touching food.
Shoppers must not take dogs into food shops.
Shoppers must not smoke in food shops.
Always be careful where you put the shopping both inside and outside of shops. Take perishable foods home quickly.

12 Don't buy frozen food if you see it lying about the shop or in a refrigerator which is too full.
Don't buy it if it feels soft.

13 All food should be put away as soon as you get home.
Perishable foods should be put into a refrigerator or cold larder. They should be used up fairly quickly.
Be careful to follow the directions on packets, etc., regarding the keeping and storing of food.
Keep all food cool, clean and covered at all times. The containers must be very clean.
The refrigerator and larder must be kept very clean and tidy.
Animals' food must never be put near human food because it can contaminate human food and cause people to be poisoned.

14 Hands must be washed before touching any food and after touching raw foods.
Chopping boards and knives, etc., must be washed after cutting up raw food.

Cuts and scratches must be properly bandaged and covered with a waterproof finger-stall.
Nobody must smoke whilst preparing or serving food.
It is safer to handle food as little as possible.
If a spoon is used for tasting it must be washed at once—preparation spoons must not be used for tasting.
Food handlers must wear clean clothes and have their hair tied back.

15 Choose foods which do not need much preparation, e.g. food to be "cooked in the bag".
Use paper handkerchiefs—once—and then put them down the lavatory or burn them. Hands should be washed every time this is done.
Never cough or sneeze into your hand, use a handkerchief.

16 The food must be cooled quickly and then put into the refrigerator.
It is better not to part-cook food, this can make it unsafe.
Don't prepare party food in advance, unless you have a refrigerator or cold store large enough to put all the food in.

17 After the oven is hot—20 minutes at Gas Mark 7, Electric 425 °F (220 °C).
On top of the stove—bring to the boil and cook for at least 15 mins.

18 Cooked meat and dishes made with meat.
Gravy, soup, homemade sauces.
Food containing gelatine.
Custard.
Real cream and artificial cream.
Ice cream.
Shell fish.
Salad foods.
Eggs, especially ducks' eggs.
Sandwiches containing meat, eggs, fish and pastes.

19 Pork and anything made with pork.

20 Separate knives and plates must be used to prepare it.
The knives and plates must be washed separately.
Pet food must never be put near human food.

21 In hot weather.
At Christmas time, at weddings and any party time.
When anybody in the home has a cold, bad throat or
intestinal illness.
They should have their own china and cutlery and these must
be washed separately, dried on a separate cloth and put in a
separate place from the other things.

22 You should complain at once. Go to another café in future.

Kitchen Safety

1 They must be—
Properly earthed.
Used with care.
Checked regularly.

2 Never leave them alone together.

3 It is not safe to do it.
The kettle lead should not be long enough to allow it.

4 No, this is not safe. The plug should always be taken out.

5 You should have dry hands.
The floor where you stand must be quite dry.

6 Turn off all cooker taps (any gas fire taps too).
When another coin is put in check all pilot lights.

7 Look to see that the burners have lit.

8 Don't leave the door open. Anybody may trip over it.
Never let small children stand on it.
Don't leave hot food on the door unattended.

9 Turn the electricity off at the main switch.

10 Have the cooker moved from the window.
Make sure the curtains are too short to catch fire, or have
no curtains or non-flare curtains.
Never put cloths on top of the stove.
Don't keep the ovencloth in the oven when not in use.

11 Pan should only be half full of fat.
Use a strong, thick, deep pan.
Don't leave the rest of the fat near the cooker.
Try not to have water boiling on the stove at the same time.
Don't leave the pan unattended.

12 Any covering which is non-slip, with no cracks or tears.
Make sure any mats are really firmly fixed.
Wipe up spills at once.

13 Store them in a safe place.
Don't leave them out when not in use.
Don't leave them on the table, etc., with the points sticking
out.
Keep them sharp. Blunt knives slip and cause accidents.
Carry knives at your side with the points downwards.

14 Keep them out of the children's way.
Never put them in any food or drink container.
Use them according to directions.
Try not to breathe them in.

15 Have the window open a little.
Use extractor fans and cooker hoods.

16 Have extra lighting over work places.
Use lights that do not throw a shadow.
Don't have the curtains too thick.

17 A wall-mounted fire, properly installed.

18 Never leave children alone in the kitchen with water, hot or
cold.
Check that the water from the hot water tap is not more than
60° C.
Keep a watch on small boilers or pans used to boil things on
the cooker.
Don't leave electric kettles on the floor to boil.
Never leave dishes of hot liquid on the edge of the table
or cooker.

19 Fire fighting equipment.
First aid equipment.

Laundry

1 At home—in the washing machine, or by hand.
Sending it to the laundry.
Taking it to the launderette.

2 (a) Prepare the clothes as follows:
Close any zips.
Tie loose apron strings, etc.
Brush off any loose dirt, e.g. from pockets.
Take off any trimmings or buttons which are not washable.
Mend tears.
Remove any bad stains which need special remover.
Empty pockets.
(b) Sort the clothes—
Sort according to the labels.
If there is not a washing label, sort according to material.

3 Because it loosens the dirt and thus saves rubbing clothes so hard they get worn out quickly.

4 Things which need to be sterilised (germs killed), e.g. nappies, handkerchiefs, bed linen, especially if somebody is ill, towels.

5 Linen and untreated cotton.

6 The wet things are kept out of the house.
They smell fresh.
Helps natural bleaching of white cotton and linen.

7 Spin driers and tumbler driers.
Drying cabinets.
Ceiling racks.
Folding frames and clothes horses.

8 To prevent mildew stains.
To protect people from chills and rheumatism caused by wearing damp clothes.

9 Outdoors—in the sunshine on a warm day.
   Indoors—in drying cabinets or airing cupboard.
         By the fire (with the guard up).

10 In a linen cupboard which is not used for airing clothes.
    Any tears in the linen should be mended before it is put away.
    Things which are not used often should be put on the top
    shelves.
    Newly washed and aired things should be put at the bottom
    of the pile.
    Damp or dirty things must never be put in the linen cupboard.

11 Read any directions first. It might be better to send the
    blanket back to the makers for cleaning.
    Choose a fine day—not too sunny.
    Shake the blankets outdoors to remove loose fluff.
    Wash in warm water and detergent, in the washing machine
    or in the sink or bath. If you use the washing machine read
    the directions given by the makers of the washing machine
    first.
    Rinse several times in warm water.
    Spin dry or squeeze gently.
    Hang out to dry, spreading the blanket out.
    Shake now and again.

12 Get advice from the clinic.
    Wash in mild soap flakes or detergent.
    Boil regularly.
    Air well.
    Any bad stains should be removed before the nappies are
    washed. Nappies should be put to soak in cold water as
    soon as they are used.
    It is important that nappies are rinsed very well indeed
    several times.

13 Look for washing instructions on the label.
    General method:
        Wash in warm water, using soap flakes or detergent.
        Wash white garments alone.
        Rinse well in warm water.
        Don't wring.
        Pat in a towel.
        Dry away from fierce heat.

14 Treat as soon as possible.
Use simple methods first, e.g. warm water, a few soap flakes, some new enzyme powders.
If you use a stain remover read the directions first.
If the article is taken to the cleaners, tell them what the stains have been caused by.

15 The stain remover must be kept locked up when not in use.
The remover must be kept in its own bottle.
Keep the label clean—pour out of the side opposite the label if the remover is the pouring kind.
Never use solvents in a closed room.
Never use inflammable solvents near a naked flame—this includes pilot lights.
Always read the directions more than once.

16 Choose a part of the article which won't show.
Wet a piece of it with water.
Squeeze in a white towel.
Lay a piece of white material over it and iron.

17 Washing machines with a wringer.
Twin tub washing machines.
Semi-automatic.
Fully automatic.
Fully automatic with tumbler drier.

18 Follow the manufacturer's directions exactly.
General method:
Empty the water out.
Disconnect the electricity supply.
Wipe all the parts.
If the rollers don't separate completely, put a piece of clean cloth between them.
Put the machine away.

19 The iron should be comfortable to hold.
It should be the right weight for the work to be done and for the person using it.
The iron should be firm when it is stood upright.
The flex should be on the correct side for the user.

20 Unplug the iron as soon as you have finished ironing.
Wipe off any marks.
If it is a steam iron, empty out any remaining water while
still hot. Stand iron on its heel.
Put it to cool, out of the reach of children.
Put it away when it's cold.
Don't wrap the flex round it.
Keep the flex in good repair, e.g. don't pull at the flex to
unplug the iron.

21 Cotton—(a) Strong wet or dry—can be soaked, scrubbed
or wrung.
Hardwearing.
Withstands high temperature for laundering.
Absorbent.
Takes dyes and special finishes easily.
Cool to wear because it allows air to pass
through it.

   (b) Laundering—White and colourfast, will boil.
Dry according to finish, e.g. drip
dry.
Starch untreated cotton.
Hot iron for damped untreated
cottons,
follow instructions for treated
cottons,
e.g. glazed.

22 Linen—(a) Strong wet or dry—can be soaked, scrubbed or
wrung.
Hardwearing.
Withstands high temperature for laundering.
Absorbent.
May be bleached or dyed.

   (b) Laundering—White and colour-fast, will boil.
Dry normally.
Starch if required.
Hot iron when very damp.

23 Wool—(a) Stretches when wet.
Feels warm and soft to touch.
Is a bad conductor of heat.
Absorbs moisture, therefore prevents body
from chilling perspiration.

Fairly elastic.

Can be made moth-proof and shrink resisting.

Can be bleached and dyed.

(b) Laundering—Measure before washing.
Use only warm water for washing and rinsing.
Don't rub, twist or soak.
Use mild soap flakes or detergent.
Press out water in a towel. Shake gently.
Dry flat or hang evenly.
If pressing is necessary, use a warm iron
and a damp cloth.

24 Silk—(a) Warm in winter and cool in summer.
Light yet strong.
Drapes well.
Is crease resistant.
Can be bleached and dyed.

(b) Laundering—Test for colour fastness first.
Check instructions, e.g. "dry cleaning only".
Use warm water and mild detergent.
Do not rub or boil or soak.
Dry away from direct heat.
Warm iron, when evenly damped.
(Wild silk is ironed dry as a rule.)
Usually better to iron silk on the wrong side.

25 Rayon—(a) Usually weaker when wet.
Drapes well.
Can be dyed.
Often a mixture of fibres.

(b) Laundering—Make sure it can be washed.
Use warm water and mild detergent.
Don't wring or rub.
Dry away from direct heat.
Warm or cool iron when damp.
Usually ironed on the wrong side.

26 Nylon—(a) Strong and hardwearing. Doesn't lose much strength when wet.
Lightweight and fairly elastic.
Crease resistant.
Mothproof.
Not affected by mildew.
Dirt resistant.
Does not shrink or stretch.
Quick drying.

(b) Laundering—Check with washing instructions.
Hand-hot water and detergent.
Rinse well.
Do not boil or bleach.
Drip dry, away from strong heat.
Warm iron, damp or dry as instructed.

27 Terylene—(a) Strong wet or dry.
Resistant to shrinking, stretching, creasing.
Mothproof.
Dirt resistant.
Quick drying.

(b) Laundering—Check with instructions.
Hand-hot water.
Rinse well.
Do not boil or bleach.
Drip-dry away from strong heat.
Warm iron, or medium hot.

28 Lycra—(a) Elastic-like material.
Good stretch and recovery.
Strong and durable.
Lightweight.
Soft.
Used mainly for foundation garments and swimwear.

(b) Laundering—Never let it get too dirty.
Wash in warm water with mild soap or detergent.
Wash white articles alone.
Rinse well.
Drip-dry away from fierce heat.
Do not iron.

29 Flame-resistant fabrics—(a) Their most important property is that they do not flare, but they may still melt and burn. These points must be checked when buying and remembered.

    (b) Laundering—Do exactly as instructed.
General rules:
Do not use soap—use a soapless detergent.
Do not boil or bleach.
Use warm water.
Cool iron when slightly damp.

30 Fibreglass—(a) Non-flammable.
Resistant to bacteria.
Drapes well.
Does not stretch, sag or shrink.
Dirt-resistant.
Mothproof.
Quick drying.

    (b) Laundering—Don't machine wash.
Don't boil or bleach.
Soak for a short while in warm water and detergent.
Rinse well.
Don't twist or rub.
Drip-dry—hang evenly.
Do not iron.

31 Launder as if the whole material was made of the weaker fibre.
E.g. cotton and rayon—wash as rayon.
Terylene and wool—wash as wool.

Money

1 "Pay as you earn."
It is the method by which Income Tax is paid weekly or monthly. The money is taken out of the worker's wages before he gets them.

2 Personal allowance.

3 Children.
Dependent relations.
Mortgage interest.
Life assurance.
Married woman's earned income.

4 The employed person and his employer both contribute
money, which is related to the employed person's wages,
to pay for the National Insurance scheme.
The money is paid at the same time as Income Tax.
This is a new system that came into being in April 1975.
People who work for themselves pay a higher contribution
than the rest of the community.

5 The cash benefits of the National Insurance scheme are paid
out for the following:
Sickness
Unemployment
Retirement
Maternity
Industrial injuries
Widows
Death.

6 You can save money through the following:
Banks
Trustee savings banks
Building societies
National (formerly Post Office) Savings Bank.

7 They provide money when it's needed.
They give people a sense of security.
They are a way of saving.

8 Life assurance.
Fire insurance.
Comprehensive insurance.
Car insurance.

9 In case of accident or illness, loss of luggage, tickets, etc.
Cancellation of holiday. Bad weather.

10 Work out a budget of how you intend to spend your money.
Keep weekly or monthly accounts of how the money is spent.

11 Read the policy carefully to make sure—
It covers all the accidents you want it to.
You will get the whole cost of putting things right.

12 Such things as:
Roads and street lighting.
Education.
Libraries and museums.
Parks and playgrounds.
Clinics.
Police and Fire Brigades.
Sewerage.

13 Ready cash.
Hire purchase.
Credit sales.
Clubs.
Budget buying.
Mail order.

14 Cheques.
Cash.
Banker's Orders.
Postal orders and money orders.
Credit cards.
Giro.

15 The advantages of Hire Purchase are as follows:
People can get things they might not be able to have otherwise.
They can get the article straight away, instead of waiting until they have saved up for it.
It is possible to get things that you can use to make money with, e.g. a knitting machine.
People can get the things they want and keep their own money, although they have to pay to do this, in the Interest.

16 The article costs more than if you bought it for cash.
It is easy to get more "H.P." than you can afford.
The thing can be worn out before it is paid for.
If a man loses his job, or the wife has to leave hers, the
H.P. payments can be a big worry if they are too large.

17 The following lend money for people to buy houses:
Building Societies.
Insurance Companies.
Some Local Authorities.
Banks.

18 By laws the Government makes.
By bodies such as:
The Consumers' Association.
The Design Council.
The British Standards Institution.
By Citizens' Advice Bureaux.
By many manufacturers who give value for money.
By good guarantees.

19 For how long is it valid?
What does it guarantee?
Who pays if the article has to be sent back?
Does the manufacturer have to pay labour costs as well as
the cost of the replacement?
Do you have to sign a card and send it back by a certain
time?
Are there any points which may mean that you do not
really get any benefit if the article is faulty?

20 Before buying things the following must be checked
carefully:
The price of the article.
Will it go into the space you have set aside for it?
Is it safe; is it strong?
Does it work well?
Is it easy to clean?
Can it be serviced and repaired? Are these costs likely
to be high?
Will somebody come and demonstrate to you how to use
the article?